KATHARINE SUSANNAH PRICHARD (1883–1969) was born in Levuka, Fiji, where her father was editor of the Fiji Times. She matriculated from South Melbourne College and worked briefly as a governess. She later taught in Melbourne studying English literature at night. In 1908 she travelled to London, working as a freelance journalist for the *Melbourne Herald* and, on her return, as the social editor of the *Herald*'s women's page. In 1912 she again left for England to pursue a career as a writer and published two novels, *The Pioneers* and *Windlestraws*. From the 1920s until her death she lived at Greenmount, Western Australia, earning her living as a writer of novels, short stories and plays. Her novels include *Black Opal, Working Bullocks, The Wild Oats of Han, Coonardoo, Haxby's Circus, Intimate Strangers*, and the Goldfields trilogy: *The Roaring Nineties, Golden Miles*, and *Winged Seeds*. Prichard was a member of the Communist Party of Australia until her death, and her political concerns were reflected in most of her published work. Her novels were published throughout the world and translated into numerous languages. In 1951 she was nominated for the Nobel Prize for Literature.

Katharine Susannah Prichard

BRUMBY INNES
+ BID ME TO LOVE
by Katharine Susannah Prichard

edited by Katharine Brisbane

Currency Press • Sydney

Brumby Innes was first published in 1940 by Paterson's Press, Perth.
This edition of *Brumby Innes* and *Bid Me To Love* first published in 1974 by Currency Methuen Drama.
Reprinted in 1983 by Currency Press Pty Ltd,
PO Box 2287, Strawberry Hills, NSW, 2012, Australia
enquiries@currency.com.au; www.currency.com.au

This edition first published by Currency Press in 2018.

Cataloguing-In-Publication data for this title is available from the National Library of Australia website: www.nla.gov.au

First published with the assistance of the Literature Board of the Australia Council.

Currency Press acknowledges the Traditional Owners of the Country on which we live and work. We pay our respects to all Aboriginal and Torres Strait Islander Elders, past and present.

Contents

Illustrations

Acknowledgements

I gratefully acknowledge the generous assistance of Mr. Ric Throssell who first brought the text of *Bid Me To Love* to my attention, and has saved me from certain errors with his kind advice. I must also thank Dr. Carl von Brandenstein, lately Reader in Anthropology at the University of Western Australia, for his uniquely valuable notes on the Aboriginal tribes of the Mount Newman area in north–western Australia; and Mr. Jonathan Shaw, who was my close collaborator on the preparation of the texts and textual notes.

Throssell family photographs are reproduced by kind permission of Mr. Ric Throssell.

Katharine Brisbane

Preface

I've just finished two plays for the *Triad* affair. One a Nor'-wester which I suppose will be considered unproduceable. But the thing wrote itself. I couldn't help it. As I saw the corroboree, it was the most thrilling and dramatic performance I've ever seen. It could be produced; but Jimmy doesn't like the play, at all. It's too brutal, he thinks. But it's true in every word and detail really. I don't in the least expect it to please anybody. And the other is an 'honest-to-God' attempt to write comedy. Jim says it isn't! So there we are.

(Katharine Susannah Prichard to Vance Palmer, 23rd June 1927.)

But *Brumby Innes* won the *Triad* Competition—and waited forty-five years for production. *Bid Me To Love*, Katharine's 'honest-to-God' comedy, was unplaced in the competition. It remained unheard of, until I found it among her papers, recognized in her comments on marriage and sexual freedom the light-hearted prophecy of Women's Liberation, and produced the play for Canberra Repertory.

Katharine Susannah Prichard did not consider herself a playwright: her place in Australian literature rests upon the twenty-four published volumes of her work and the translation of her major novels and short stories into some fifteen foreign languages. Yet she wrote seventeen plays, eleven of which were produced by the little theatres and amateur companies which were Australia's only indigenous theatre at the time. And *Brumby Innes*, when in 1972 it at last reached the public in John Smythe's production for the Australian Performing Group and the Nindethana Company at the Pram Factory, Melbourne, was greeted with enthusiasm by the critics. Barrie Watts wrote in the *Australian*:

> Anyone thinking of putting indigenous ingredients together and writing The Great Australian Play can screw the cap back on his pen and take himself off quietly to the pub. It has been belatedly discovered that Katharine Susannah Prichard wrote it in 1927.[1]

The theatre was a part of her childhood. Her father, Tom Prichard, editor of the *Fiji Times*, was an enthusiastic amateur actor. An imposing Jason with an incongruous walrus moustache, crimson cloak, short blue tunic and discreet white lace above the knees, he still challenges me from a dusty water-colour on the wall of my workroom. Katharine tells of her own youthful exploits in the story of her childhood, *The Wild Oats of Han*: how she found the *Plays of William Shakespeare* in the forbidden sanctuary of her father's study and lay full length on the floor gazing at the pictures, absorbed in her own story-making, content to let her parents believe that she had been reading the plays when they discovered her:

> 'I believe, dear, our harum-scarum will be a credit to us after all,' her father said...
> 'You will be asked for reminiscences of her childhood when she has become famous and you will say: "She was intelligent always—read Shakespeare at the age of nine—although a sore trial to her parents at most times."'

Or how she dressed in her mother's opera cloak and corsets and a pair of lavender tights from her father's theatrical box and played 'Mademoiselle Delicia', the circus queen, in a death-defying leap from the branches of a willow tree to fall winded into the garden, cured for the time of theatrical ambition.

Her first attempt at play writing was no more encouraging. She had dramatised the story of William Tell and determined to produce the play for her family and friends. Katharine remembered her first excursion into drama in the autobiography, *Child of the Hurricane*, when at eighty she retraced the years. She had written out all the parts for her brothers and cousins, coaxed them unavailingly to learn their lines, and carefully devised the stage effects. But before a delighted audience of relatives and neighbours things went sadly wrong. Kattie found herself not only playing the part of Tell's wife, but moving as unobtrusively as she could from character to character, whispering their lines. And when at the critical moment the bolt was fired, young Tell forgot to pull the hidden string. The apple remained securely balanced on his head until a harassed producer raced across the stage to remind him. The apple fell in neat halves, but abandoning their parts, Tell and his son both dived for a half of the apple. The audience wept with laughter.

'It's not everybody who can write a play and produce it, and make the costumes and play all the parts,' a friend of her father's consoled her.

Undeterred, Katharine decided at fifteen, after seeing *Henry V* with George Rignold in the lead, that she would become an actress; and she did once appear with the Yarram Dramatic Society in the title role of Pinero's *Sweet Lavender*. But by that time the all-absorbing determination to become a writer had replaced her youthful ambition for the stage.

Katharine told me once that her first ambition was to write for the theatre; but she was already embarked upon her career as a freelance journalist, with a handful of published short stories to her credit, when her first one-act play, *The Burglar*, was produced at the Australian Drama Night arranged by William Moore and Louis Esson in Melbourne in 1909. The play, a slight comedy on a conventional theme, is significant only in that it is the first evidence of a stirring social conscience which was to be a central part of Katharine Prichard's later writing. A young woman socialist (one of the first socialist heroines to find her way into the theatre) disturbs a burglar in her bedroom and presents him with the treasured trinkets and heirlooms given to her by her mother and father, to help 'pay his way' through University. 'I was in such a blasted hurry to be an ornament of respectable society,' the burglar explains. The girl replies:

And I am always in a hurry to bestow myself out of what is called 'respectable society'. Do you know there is nothing more unrespectable than so-called respectable society. Really it's a caucus of people who never think, and are stupid and cruel to those who do, who wear their beliefs like their skin and cannot understand that what we believed yesterday we don't today, or won't tomorrow…

But parting with her treasured mementoes has all been a pretence, to conceal the diamonds left in her keeping by her fiance. 'The wretched useless things! How I hate them,' she exclaims and bursts into passionate tears.

Two short curtain–raisers written for the Actresses' Franchise League during a six-year residence in London followed. *Her Place*, produced in 1913, comments mildly on the class consciousness of the English. The plot uses the same symbols of wealth and privilege employed in the earlier play, and later echoed in the London-based romance, *Windlestraws*. A valuable pearl necklace has been stolen. In order to avoid incriminating a flighty young boarder, the charwoman accepts the blame herself. Exonerated, she explains:

> There was me an old woman, Miss, with all me life be'ind me... And there w's 'er, a young girl, with all 'ers before er... I 'opes I knows my place.

With a somewhat delayed attack of conscience, her employer puts the moral of the piece:

> Do you think she knows her place, Pete? Look at her hands. And her eyes. She'd have gone to gaol for Rosalie—who isn't even grateful! Do you know, Bunny dear, the place for selfish and idle women like her and me, is at the feet of women like you. And your place is on a pedestal...

No copy of the second London play survives; but it was reported in the Melbourne *Herald*'s account of a reception to delegates to a conference on Women's Suffrage.[2] Katharine Susannah, it seems, had discovered the agitprop:

> The *pièce de résistance* was a stirring dramatic sketch, *For Instance*, written especially for the occasion by Miss K. Prichard (Melbourne) and the scene of which was a room in a white blouse factory in Australia. In this work the writer showed a rare skill in compacting together romance, politics and social economics. For it was designedly 'a play with a purpose', turning upon the very much better fortune than any she had hitherto known which comes to an English factory girl who goes to Australia, whither she had been assisted by a Government lady in the Strand. So propagandist indeed is the whole thing that while listening one almost suspected that our astute immigration officials had been using Miss Prichard's brain to 'improve the occasion'.

A third play written in London, *A Miracle in the Street of Refugees*, remained unproduced. Towards the end of her life Katharine revised it slightly and sent it to Leslie Rees at the Australian Broadcasting Commission, hoping that it might be suitable for television.

Katharine Susannah Prichard returned to Australia in 1916. The long battle to win recognition abroad was won. With *The Pioneers* prize as her trophy and the satisfaction of success in the tough field of freelance journalism, her attention turned to her goal of 'knowing the Australian people and interpreting them to themselves'.

> I wanted to live and write in Australia about the country and its people. Those years in London only strengthened my desire to do so.[3]

The Pioneers was twice filmed: in 1916 by Franklyn Barret and in 1926 by Raymond Longford for Australian Films Ltd. In 1923 Katharine wrote a one-act version of an incident from the novel for the first season of the Pioneer Players in Melbourne. At Louis Esson's insistence, she later re-wrote it as a three-act play. It could not contain the full compass of the material and Katharine herself was dissatisfied with the result.[4] It remains as an affirmation of her sympathy for the underdog and faith in Australia: 'This country will be the Redeemer... blot out all the old stains,' Mary Cameron, the play's heroine, promises.

There was little time for serious dramatic writing, but often Katharine explored new ideas in a play, turned to the compression of incident and character which dramatic form demanded before embarking on the fuller score of a novel. With plays, as with poetry, those 'inconspicuous murmurings of me to myself', she sometimes spoke more directly of personal things than she allowed herself to do in her major work.

The Great Man, a comedy of the trials of parenthood, was written in 1923, shortly after my own birth in Greenmount, Western Australia, where my mother and father, Captain Hugo (Jim) Throssell V.C., had made their home. It too was presented by the Pioneer Players, before Louis Esson's short-lived experiment in a playwright's theatre collapsed, as so many of its successors did in later years. Revising the play in 1959 before presenting it to the Campbell Howard Collection at the University of New England, Katharine scrawled in pencil on the title page of the first version, 'a poor thing in my opinion'; but there was a certain simple charm about the original which was lost in her attempt to give the play contemporary relevance to the post-war housing shortage, reversing the young mother's initial revolt against middle-class domesticity and the overweening amiability of relatives:

Imagining it's more important to dust a book than read it... washing on Mondays, cleaning silver on Fridays, fretting ourselves to death if the kitchen table's not white and the saucepans haven't shiny bottoms... letting the house grow like a shell on our backs.

Katharine had already planned her next work, an allegorical novel of a broken-backed circus girl's courageous charade in the *circus maximus* of life, when she decided to visit a cattle station in the North West. *Fay's Circus*, as the book was first to be called, was intended to be her entry for the *Bulletin*'s 1928 Novel Competition. There was no thought of a play in her mind, but there was a story that she had to follow: an Aboriginal woman mustering cattle had thrown her baby into a dry creek bed and left it to die. Katharine wanted to understand how a fellow human being could be brought to such terrible madness.[5]

At Turee Creek station, three hundred miles beyond the railway at Meekatharra, on a tributary of the Ashburton River, the drama of man's conflict with the harsh, sun-blasted country absorbed her. 'It's terrifically hot—and the dust storms suffocating,' she wrote to Vance and Nettie Palmer on 19th October 1926:

But I've been riding nearly every day, and am the colour of red mulga and henna-ed with dust. Sometimes one of the gins rides with me, sometimes mine host, who is really a bit of the country, and sometimes Mick, a stockman who has lived here all his life.

And in a post-script she added:

I've done a play to be called 'The Brumby', or 'Brumby ———' somebody or other. The real thing is here. His name is Leake. It fits so—'Brumby Leake'. And I've got to find one that won't run me in for libel.

Katharine entered *Brumby Innes* for the *Triad* Competition without much hope of success. Louis Esson was the playwright and Vance Palmer, too, had more experience in the theatre. She wrote to Vance Palmer:

'Strike me breath', Vance dear, I'd give anything for you or Louis to win this stunt. Not that it counts much in itself but that it opens the door.

But when the results of the competition were announced, *Brumby Innes* was unanimously selected by the three judges from 107 entries. Gregan McMahon submitted a special report on the winning play:

> I consider *Brumby Innes* to be in a class by itself. In originality of subject, atmosphere, characterization, virility and technique, it is a very remarkable work, comparable to some of the best of Eugene O'Neill's, and it is, more-over, essentially Australian. It has been objected that the subject matter is sordid, and on that account the possibility of production should be discouraged. I am assuming that the subject matter of the plays presented is no concern of the judges: it matters not whether it be sordid tragedy or bedroom farce. We are looking for an Australian playwright who has the gift and the technique of playmaking, who can at the same time work with facility in a purely Australian atmosphere, and from whom, in the future, work of a high standard may be expected. If the playwriting competition brings to light such a one, I think he should be placed first, irrespective of his medium. In my opinion, we have found him in the author of *Brumby Innes*.

Tait's were to produce the prize-winning play, but despite Gregan McMahon's intention to create a special company to present *Brumby Innes*, it remained unperformed until, in a more tolerant time, Australians could look with maturity and understanding at their own past. In 1927, even to Louis Esson, *Brumby lines* was immoral and shocking:

> Apart altogether from its literary and dramatic quality, I didn't think *Brumby Innes* had a possible chance. It is a powerful and picturesque work, beginning with a wonderful corroboree, but the episodes are startling enough to make most people shudder. A Repertory or any other audience will get the shock of their lives when it is played. A few cuts may be made, of course, but nothing can prevent it being a terribly daring play. It has some splendid scenes and characters, and you are made to feel the atmosphere of a wild and lonely cattle station of the

Nor'-west; but personally I think the author has been too sympathetic to Brumby. Nothing can excuse his brutality, not even his 'virility', which is his long suit. Kattie says she had written a short last act but did not include it. It seems to me another act or scene is necessary. Another ending might give a better twist to the moral. But it is a good and hopeful thing that a real Australian play should be chosen instead of a cheap bit of bogus romance. It is the type of play the Pioneers should have done. Its influence, dramatic if not moral, will be good. It is a notable contribution to a future Australian repertoire, and would create a stir anywhere.[6]

Brumby Innes did not come to life until three years after Katharine Susannah Prichard died, but Brumby himself was re-created in the form of Sam Geary of *Coonardoo*, when the searing intensity of inspiration could no longer be denied and the novel streamed from her pen in a surge of creative energy to sweep up the *Bulletin* novel prize in 1928.

Katharine returned to the softer setting of Greenmount in autumn and the domestic theme in *Bid Me To Love*, a simple comedy of the days before farce lost its separate identity on the stage. It is a play which draws its humour from observed reality; which finds gentle amusement in the frailty of its characters and the contradictions between their romantic ideals and their very ordinary impulses and inhibitions.

To me the reality of the setting and characters of the play was transparent. The verandah of our home at Greenmount was described in the stage directions; my father spoke in Greg's every word; I saw my mother's romanticism and unconventionality in Louise; found my own childish sayings recalled; even Phoebus Apollo, the family cat, was included in the cast. As to the plot—fact, or fiction to tease her own Jim? That remains K.S.P.'s private joke.

Margaret Williams wrote recently:

> *Brumby Innes* is not first and foremost about white exploitation of black, but about the nature of sexual relationships, and is really a hard-headed demolishing of the whole concept of romantic love as a basis for sexuality.[7]

In a way, *Bid Me To Love* turns the coin. It glances with amusement at the marriage contract—and its problematic alternatives.

Katharine Susannah Prichard pictured in the 1920s on the terrace of the Throssell family home at Greenmount, Western Australia—the setting for Bid Me To Love.

Brumby Leake (extreme left) in 1932, then aged 67, with friends. Jim Edwards (second from right) is believed to have been a model for Jim Hallinan. Photo in the possession of Dr. Richard Maguire.

Below: The homestead (now no longer in use) occupied by Brumby Leake at Prairie Downs station, which adjoins Turee Creek station to the east. Photo by kind permission of Mrs. P. Bondini.

As *Brumby Innes* foreshadows the fuller score of *Coonardoo*, *Bid Me To Love* anticipates in many ways the novel *Intimate Strangers*, which had tragic parallels in Katharine's own life.[8] The names of the principal characters are the same (in the early notes for the novel Elodie, too, is called Louise). The theme remains marriage, clouded in the novel with the racking reality of the Great Depression.

Under the financial stress and political ferment of the 'thirties, Katharine saw literature as playing a more direct role in 'the battle for or against'. Her later plays reflect this decision. An unproduced play, *The Great Strike*, written on internal evidence in 1931 or 1932, tells in the first act of a miners' strike at Broken Hill, and in a political science fiction conclusion foresees worker control of the mines. *Forward One*, a one-act play written in support of striking shop assistants, was produced by the Workers Art Guild in Perth in 1935. *Women of Spain*, a passionate appeal for assistance for embattled Republican Spain, followed in 1937.

Penalty Clause, later re-titled *Solidarity*, was the longest and most successful of Katharine's agitprop plays. It told of a strike of miners on the West Australian gold-fields when one of their mates is killed in a fall of rock in a dangerous section of the mine, despite the loss of holiday pay under the so-called penalty clauses of the then existing industrial legislation. The play was produced by the Workers Art Guild for the 1940 West Australian Drama Festival. Paul Hasluck, then drama critic for the *West Australian*, found the play unconvincing in its industrial advocacy but moving in its presentation of human problems:

> The chief reason for the human strength of the play, however, was the writer's genius and the sympathy and understanding which fed it. If she is content with having revealed something of the human situations which lie behind industrial relations and the ways in which negotiations proceed, her play is a signal success. It has given suffering flesh and eager blood to workers and their wives and sweethearts. And it was this human quality in the play that was most convincingly reproduced in the strikingly natural presentation by the Workers Art Guild.[9]

In the war years, all of Katharine Susannah Prichard's energy was directed towards the defeat of fascism. The time that was left was wholly absorbed in the immense goldfields trilogy covering three generations of men and women, over a span of some fifty years. The final volume was published in 1950. Exhausted, and disillusioned by the reaction of critics who saw the work as mere propaganda, Katharine's unresting creative impulse turned again to drama. In 1951, she completed a long biographical drama on Alfred Deakin, the founder of Australian Federation, who had once been a friend of her father's. The play was entered in the Commonwealth Jubilee Stage Play competition of that year. When Katharine learnt that the competition had been won by Kylie Tennant with a play on the same subject, *Tether a Dragon*, she was at first suspicious of Miss Tennant's treatment of Deakin; but after reading the play, she allowed her own material to remain unproduced and unpublished.

Katharine returned to comedy in her final play, *Persephone's Baby*, the story of the baby son of her friend, Sumner Locke, who died in child-birth in London leaving her baby to be brought up by three sisters in the helter-skelter world of the theatre. (Sumner Locke Eliot later wrote the story of his childhood in the novel, *Careful, He Might Hear You*.) Katharine had urged me to collaborate in the play, to give my own hopes as a playwright a leg-up. I was unenthusiastic, and Katharine herself regarded the play as 'just a piece of confectionery'. She wrote in February 1959:

> I'll never try to write another play. It's not my medium. Doesn't interest me enough—too many inhibitions, and outlines rather than filling in a character—nuances which have to be left to actors and producers...

Persephone's Baby was entered in a national play competition, nevertheless, under my name, with K. Throssell as collaborator. 'You needn't be associated, if we don't get anywhere,' Katharine wrote to me. I had entered a play of my own, and for once in my life was glad when both scripts were returned without comment.

In her monograph on Katharine Susannah Prichard,[10] Henrietta Drake-Brockman quotes an article in *The Realist* (No. 14, 1964) in which Katharine, anxious that I should succeed unshadowed by her fame, said:

I gave up writing plays when Ric began to demonstrate more dramatic talent than I had.

Her own little-known contribution to Australian drama, briefly surveyed in these pages, has its place in the stream which leads to the great spring flood of Australian dramatic writing in the seventies.[11]

Ric Throssell
Canberra, 1973

Introduction

Katharine Susannah Prichard

Katharine Susannah Prichard's present place in Australian literature is that of a novelist and short story writer. Her novels are characterised by her concern to improve the lot of the ordinary Australian and by her lyrical evocation of country life—the opal fields in *Black Opal*, the timber country in *Working Bullocks*, the country town circuit in *Haxby's Circus*, the cattle country in *Coonardoo* and the goldfields in her trilogy: *The Roaring Nineties*, *Golden Miles* and *Winged Seeds*.

She was born of Australian parents in Levuka, Fiji, in 1883, one of four children. Her father was editor of the *Fiji Times*. They moved soon after to Launceston and later to Melbourne where she was educated at South Melbourne College. She became a governess in Gippsland and Broken Hill, and then a journalist in Melbourne. In 1909 she spent a year in Britain and there first explored Fabianism and other current socialist thought. On her return she became a staff journalist on the Melbourne *Herald* and at this time she wrote her first play, *The Burglar*. Just before the outbreak of war she returned to Britain as a freelance journalist and there wrote her first novel, *The Pioneers*, set in Gippsland. It won a Hodder and Stoughton £1,000 prize and was published in 1915. In 1919 after her return home she married Captain Hugo Vivian Hope Throssell, V.C. and they went to live in Greenmount, in the Darling Ranges outside Perth, where she lived until her death in 1969. Their son Ric was born in 1922. Hugo Throssell died by his own hand in 1934.

The earliest literary influence she felt was that of the English, French and German classics; but several aspects of her early life were a continuing influence upon her writing. Her Fijian nurse, she suggests in the autobiographical *Child of the Hurricane*, gave her a natural sympathy with her Aboriginal characters like Coonardoo. The industrial troubles of the 'nineties affected her profoundly, costing her father his working life when the *Daily Telegraph*, of which he was

xxii   INTRODUCTION

Tasmanian editor, ceased publication. For many years he contributed a current affairs column to the *Age*, which towards the end Katharine Prichard ghosted. His disappointment and failing health gave her a bitter independence as an adolescent. Finally, there was the influence of a circle of litterateurs which included Louis and Hilda Esson, Vance and Nettie Palmer, William Moore and Guido Barracchi. She shared with them the left–wing sympathies common among intellectuals in the 'twenties and 'thirties and a strong belief that Australians should have a genuine literary voice. She also shared their classical education and intense isolation in a climate which afforded, generally, very little lively critical appreciation of the kind they had encountered in Europe; and she shared, too, their deep dependence upon each other, which made sensitivities tender in, for example, the incident of the prize awarded in 1927 by the literary journal *Triad*.

The struggles of a conservative and orthodox family reduced to making ends meet, her own battle to make an independent living as a writer, the hunger marches she saw in London in 1909 and the wartime suffering she saw on her second visit to Britain—these were lasting harsh influences upon Katharine Prichard's writing, and her public response was to join the Communist Party of Australia when it was formed in 1920. But overall the 'twenties, with which this book is concerned, found her in a gentler setting—that of *Bid Me To Love*—which elicited her romantic and sensual qualities, her pleasure in comfort and natural beauty. Her son was born, she took a trip with a circus troupe to gather material for *Haxby's Circus*, and another to Turee Creek Station, where she found Brumby and Coonardoo.

ii
Brumby Innes *and* Coonardoo

Brumby Innes is a remarkable document. Begun at remote Turee Creek Station, completed in the isolation of Katharine Susannah Prichard's home, and running starkly against the taste of the day, it was written without reference to any theatre and without prospect of performance (as it proved) in her lifetime; yet it runs with the economy and surefootedness of natural dramatic writing, and with the urgency and honesty which make—as we now have a chance to assess—lasting drama. Ric Throssell points out that Katharine Susannah Prichard wrote seventeen plays—a major commitment to the theatre. A number of them have been lost; some of them were performed by amateur social and literary groups; but the theatre itself contributed nothing to her growth as a playwright. This has been the experience of very many Australian writers who have been drawn to the theatre but found their fulfilment as writers of prose fiction: Vance Palmer, for example, Dymphna Cusack, Patrick White, Henrietta Drake–Brockman. Katharine Prichard had a particular daring, a particular sense of the romantic and the dramatic which in other circumstances could have made her literary fame primarily as a dramatist.

Brumby Innes and *Bid Me To Love* make an interesting pair to bed in one volume. They were written at the same time and both entered for the *Triad* prize. *Brumby Innes* won and *Bid Me To Love* received no mention, which is as it should be. The former contains a much larger, braver, more individual, more reverberating statement. And yet they need to be read as a pair, for they each reflect light upon the other.

Bid Me To Love illuminates the city life to which Brumby's May has been bred, with its "advanced" ideas and its protected lives, its free but unchallenged class system; and Brumby Innes, hovering in the background of Louise, casts a shadow upon her sophistication, demonstrating how the urban Australian has transformed his acres, barricaded himself against the strange, raw, barbaric land which proclaims its own standard of morality and survival; and which Brumby himself embraces with a poetic reality which has a truth deeper and in its way purer than the literary ideologies of Louise. That Katharine Prichard, writing so close to her immediate experience, was able to recognise the sober facts, makes her a writer of considerable calibre.

Brumby Innes opens with a corroboree, in its way a clear challenge to the theatre of Katharine Prichard's time or any time to acknowledge its duty to realise the author's vision. The opening scene is brief and dramatic and it introduces vividly the qualities of her style: the romantic tempered with realism, the poetic disciplined with dedicated accuracy, the novelistic heightened with dramatic economy. The text begins as might one of her novels:

Under a wide stretch of starlit sky, native women and children are sitting in two rows at a little distance from the camp fire.

Her directions are precise and practical; but with a generosity of detail which betrays the writer determined to commit to the page every last detail of the picture in her mind.

History has proved her right, if caution was her motive; for the play was first performed three thousand miles and two generations away from its native habitat, in the urban heart of Melbourne, by an Aboriginal theatre group and a white theatre group, each as innocent as the other of any experience of the South–Pandjima tribe or of a part of Australia long since transformed beyond recognition. The playwright is very free with her stage directions. There is hardly a speech without an adverb in parenthesis, instructing the actor—evidence again of her desire to realise the whole performance as one can in a novel. For she had no experience of the real theatre's creative use of a text. Had the play taken its place in an established native theatre before publication, it is unlikely that many of these directions would have survived into the text. The text in this volume is the author's revision of the play as first published in 1940. But while the stage directions reflect the prevailing air of uncertainty about the theatre for which Katharine Prichard was writing, there is nothing unsure about her dialogue. The lines are finely honed and rise from within the characters with the true insight of a realist writer.

In her novel, *Coonardoo*, written shortly after *Brumby Innes*, several of the same characters and references appear; Karrara Station, Cecil Grant and Cock–Eyed Bob are common to both works. Brumby Innes was inspired by the drover and stockman Brumby Leake, a character renowned in the Kimberleys and who spent his last years at Prairie Downs Station, which adjoins Turee Creek to the east. A photograph of his homestead, preserved much as it was in his time, is reproduced here. In *Coonardoo* Sam Geary is identifiably Brumby Innes. The attitude of the author, however, is different. He interests her, but at a distance; he haunts the young station owner, Hugh, stockily real but none the less the villain of the book, watching and waiting for a chance to bring about the downfall of both Hugh and Coonardoo.

Here is the climactic confrontation between Coonardoo and Geary:

Geary came along the verandah. He lurched against the door of the
room she was in, and the door opened. Coonardoo hung powerless
before him. Heavy and drunken, in the doorway, his eyes glazed,
Geary stood, swaying, an old man with his hair on end, his face red,
swollen and ugly. Coonardoo could have moved past and away from
him in the darkness. But she did not move. As weak and fascinated as a
bird before a snake, she swayed there for Geary whom she had loathed
and feared beyond any human being. Yet male to her female, she could
not resist him. Her need of him was as great as the dry earth's for rain.[1]

There follows a description of the morning calm after the storm:

By midday they were ready for the road again. Geary was rather in a
hurry to be off before Hugh came in. He was uneasy in his mind about
how Hugh would regard the French leave he had taken with his house
and women—particularly Coonardoo. Although over that he had got
rather a shock. Drunk he had been, but not so drunk he did not hear and
understand Coonardoo when she cried to herself, "Youie not want 'm!"

Sam was curious to know why she said that. Coonardoo had told
him.

In the morning, before he left the verandah, Geary called
Coonardoo. She came from the kitchen and stood before him. "Come
and be my woman, Coonardoo," he said. "I'll treat you better than
Youie does. Give you silk gina–ginas, necklaces—a wristlet watch."

Coonardoo's eyes flashed their anger and loathing. Very straight
and dignified, her eyes took Sam Geary's. She turned her back on him
and walked away.

The implications of the triangular relationship are clear in this passage,
the impulses behind the actions are carefully considered by the author.
But in the writing they are nowhere as passionately observed as they
are in *Brumby Innes*. Defiant though she was, Katharine Prichard's
boldness was tempered with a certain fastidiousness in her novels (and
indeed, as it was, the contemporary reaction to *Coonardoo* showed
she had overstepped the mark of current 'community standards'). But
Bruinby Innes, perhaps because of its remote production prospects, she
seems to have written for herself. And dramatic writing, by its bony
economy, allows for no descriptive relief, no moral directives, no
change of course. By its nature it worries out coyness, demands in the

flesh and blood of the actor the flesh and blood of the characters. And in *Brumby Innes* Katharine Prichard answers the challenge. Take the end of Act Two:

> BRUMBY: They call me the brumby.
>
> MAY: [*frightened but fencing*] I've heard what a wonderful bushman you are.
>
> BRUMBY: You have, have you? [*With easy conceit*] Well, that's right. I've knocked round with gins all me days: gins and bullocks, blacks and brumbies. Born in the Breakaway country. Never been to school. But I want a white woman. How about stayin' here?
>
> MAY: [*coquettishly, thinking she has the reins again*] It's awfully sweet of you to ask me, but—
>
> BRUMBY: [*throwing an arm round her and holding her*] You been foolin' all the men you've set eyes on up here, for the last six months. You aren't goin' to fool me.
>
> MAY: Let me go.
>
> BRUMBY: [*laughing*] Not on your life.
>
> MAY: If you don't…
>
> BRUMBY: Well?
>
> MAY: I'll scream the place down.
>
> BRUMBY: Scream away. They wouldn't hear you at the yards… even if I let you.
>
> MAY: [*struggling, but yielding*] Oh you…
>
> BRUMBY: [*laughing triumphantly and embracing her roughly, as he pushes her towards the bunk*] I like 'em thoroughbred and buckin' a bit at first.

There is no way by which the author in this context can disengage herself from the characters. It is admirably dramatic, expressing itself freely and assuredly in the choice of words and rhythms: Brumby's bluntness, May's floundering archness; and through both a confident humour, replacing the earnestness of the novel. Within an economy unique to the theatre Katharine Prichard creates a scene which is overtly theatrical in its excitement and at the same time anchors the characters firmly in their background and divides our sympathy between both. Brumby is the aggressor but there is no implied moral judgement. On the contrary, of the two he is the honest one. May is the victim, and yet her ignorant sexuality is shown up for the shallow, resourceless thing it is.

This sequence is an example of the qualities which make *Brumby Innes* an exceptional piece in the context of Katharine Prichard's work. Another is the shape and rhythm of the structure. Music was important in Katharine Prichard's life and is used as an emotional reference on many occasions in her novels. *Brumby Innes* has an orchestration which is quite distinctive, beginning as it does with the songs of the corroboree, in which we hear the rising rhythms of the dance broken by the rude intrusion of the drunken Brumby. In the second act the white men's 'corroboree' as they exchange their own folk tales over the whisky bottle explodes into the verses of *Shift Boys, Shift*. This sound is superseded by the screams of the black girl Wylba (the cause of the previous ruckus), who is locked in the storeroom.

The third act opens in silence, slow lethargic lines reflecting the change that has taken place in May, and punctuated by the low wailing of the blind Tullamurra. The action rises towards its resolution with the advent of Brumby and ends with the defeat of May. Wylba and Brumby dance happily to the gramophone—the black and white stepping in unison to the music of a modern music maker as domestic as the opening corroboree is pagan.

Each act is carefully structured, not in terms of action, in a manner to be defined as 'well–made', but as reflecting in the rise and fall of the rhythms the characters themselves. The beginning of each act sets a tempo which anticipates the emotional statement of the act. Each act ends with Brumby at the business of taming his mares.

Finally *Brumby Innes* is remarkable because it is so essentially itself. At a time when European literature and European music set Australian standards of perfection, Katharine Prichard felt close enough to the black women Polly and Wylba to see them with a woman's sympathy, and was attracted enough to the music and language of the South–Pandjima tribe to pay them the tribute of depicting them as accurately as, with her experience, she could. Dr. Carl von Brandenstein has made a specialist study of this area of the Kimberleys, and gives elsewhere in this book a detailed analysis of the tribal language used in the play. He points out that, understandably, Katharine Prichard's grasp of the rituals and the dialect of the South–Pandjima was not that of a native to the Kimberleys, nor that of an anthropologist. It is simpler than that—a natural womanly response to her environment, unusual in the literature of the nineteen–twenties.

Brumby Innes was half a century ahead of its time in the values it gives to romance and sexuality; and it retains its sense of surprise because the values expressed are the author's, born freshly from her stay in the Breakway country, and owing little to popular fashion.

D. H. Lawrence, who had visited Perth only five years before and whose close affinity with the natural world was already influential, was the writer most in sympathy with her at the time. Katharine Prichard did not care for comparisons with Lawrence:

> I admired *Sons and Lovers* immensely when it was written and had read most of Lawrence's other books, not with the same enthusiasm. *Kangaroo* was a bitter disappointment despite lovely descriptive passages, perhaps because I had expected so much from it. In *Aaron's Rod*, which Lawrence sent me, I found again the qualities which I admired in his writing; but our philosophies were too far apart for my mind to have been influenced by his style and outlook, as has sometimes been suggested. At the same time, I think Lawrence had a liberating effect on most of the writers of my generation.[2]

By 1937, three years after the death of her husband, when she published *Intimate Strangers*, she had put aside the world of *Brumby Innes*. But in 1927 the affinity is vividly her greatest strength.

iii
Bid Me To Love *and* Intimate Strangers

Intimate Strangers is the novel closest to *Bid Me To Love*. It revolves round Greg and Elodie Blackwood and the circle of friends at their beach cottage, Ywurrie, near Perth. Elodie is a Jewish pianist who gave up her promising career in Vienna to marry a dashing returned soldier. The story is taken up fifteen years after their marriage on the eve of the Depression, their hopes faded, and Greg about to lose his job. Greg falls in love with a frigid young mermaid called "Dirk" Hartog and Elodie with Dirk's darkly romantic cousin Jerome Hartog, a sea captain. Dirk is awakened from her class–conscious sexlessness by socialism and an Italian fisherman with whom she shares a common bond in the sea; Elodie flirts with the idea of sailing away with Jerome to a life of adventure; but the moment of truth comes when Greg despairingly attempts suicide. The book ends with Elodie and Greg somewhat improbably drawing together, as many couples did in the nineteen–twenties, to work for a new and better world through socialism.

The pair in *Bid Me To Love* are Greg and Louise: Ric Throssell tells us that in the first draft Elodie Blackwood was called Louise; their children bear the same names—Bill and Peg. The autobiographical material in both works has been remarked upon. But the political discussion which overlays the latter part of the novel is a new departure from its real strength, the study of marriage and sensuality. "Every woman of forty needs a lover to keep her self–respect—and her husband's," says Louise, elegantly flirting with Woodbridge. It is the same advice given to Elodie by a sophisticated friend,[3] with more sober consequences.

There is a real division in the novel: Katharine Prichard has said that it was intended to be a study of the effects of the Depression upon the middle class. The end was changed following the personal tragedy of her husband's death.

Bid Me To Love is a lighter thing than *Intimate Strangers* but like *Brumby Innes* it presents its characters and its time unselfconsciously and without the reforming zeal to be found in the companion novel. Again there is more humour: Louise's adventure with her Italian gardener is a *jeu d'esprit*, something born of boredom and her husband's suspected infidelity—a brief escape in a friendly bushland. "You're like a beautiful brown moth that has blown into my life," she says. May would like to have made Brumby such an adventure but she is too far out of her element; the women are sisters in their unknowing sophistication. From the safe surroundings of the Reed's cultivated garden Louise is able to play with her moth and send him away when the game is over. As Woodbridge says: "With blazes, primitive passions... you never know where you are."

In essence *Bid Me To Love* is a charming game played with the ideas more darkly used by D. H. Lawrence. It opens gently a cornucopia of the good things of nature—breakfasts of mushrooms on the terrace to the sound of magpies, and the smell of apples rising from the orchard. Don, the romantic Italian orchardist, is singing, he flings an apple over the balcony and comes to Louise bearing her children and a dark, rare moth. John Maine Woodbridge, a former lover, now a successful playwright home from abroad, appears, drunk on the forgotten smell of bushfires. His unexpected arrival gives Louise opportunity to express her advanced ideas on sexual freedom and the 'sensible' agreement she made with Greg when they married. Something, clearly, is ripe to bursting; and the full–bodied Louise is the prize fruit.

The opening of *Intimate Strangers* has no such promise of contentment. The marriage is jaded and Elodie is worn with child–rearing and the loss of her artistic promise. But in 1927 the shadow of the Great Depression had not crossed Louise's consciousness. This contented, unawakened life as it existed in the 'twenties is most delicately portrayed by Katharine Prichard, with an accuracy which today we can place in perspective. It is the more poignant because with hindsight we know that within two years the innocence which until then had characterised our kind of civilisation, had been betrayed forever by the collapse of the economy on the other side of the Pacific. In *Intimate Strangers* that innocence has become ignorance: Elodie's and Greg's primitive passions emerge as false romanticism and their friend Chrissie Field's flapper–sophistication ends in death by abortion. The heart has been betrayed and the head must take command.

In *Bid Me To Love* the music rises out of the landscape, as it does in *Brumby Innes*. It introduces Don, it supplies sympathy with Louise, it points up delicately her final shallowness, and it draws the play to an end in a half–nostalgic, half–wry conclusion which sums up the mood of the play.

> Then as the sunflow'r looks up to the light,
> Sad in its absence and glad in its sight,
> I can look up to thee, morning and night,
> And love thee forever, love thee forever and ever.

Tony the fisherman also has a song, which echoes through *Intimate Strangers*:

> More love, or more disdain, I crave
> Sweet, be not still indifferent,
> Oh, send me meekly to my grave,

Or else afford me more content,
Or love, or hate me, more or less,
For love abhors all lukewarmness.[4]

The loss of innocence can be seen even here.

Brumby Innes and *Bid Me To Love* appear, on Ric Throssell's evidence, to have been written concurrently, or at least within months of each other. Each is about what happens when one dabbles with sexual passion, each action is drawn very precisely from the landscape and in neither case does that passion disturb the *status quo*. Brumby rides on, with May a victim to that landscape; Louise and Greg ride on a little more sedately in their well–cut jodhpurs. Don is left to sing his song in solitude. The plays have, though worlds apart, a common sense of dedication to those worlds. The fact that they could, within the same period, create two such different perspectives on sexual morality perhaps stems from the author's eye for journalistic documentation.

Bid Me To Love is freer of stage directions than *Brumby Innes* —the setting of course was more familiar. There are certain roughnesses in the text which could have been polished had there been in Katharine Prichard's lifetime her kind of theatre. (In Act One, for example, Louise tells us that the express goes at eight next evening; later Greg tells Don, "Better leave about eight, I suppose.") Looking at the plays today it is clear that she was a natural dramatist, expressing herself easily from within the characters' heads with a greater freedom than she sometimes felt as a novelist. It is interesting that in both cases she chose first to express herself in dramatic form and only secondly in the novel—and to me the plays outshine the novels in their directness. We lost a most distinctive dramatist when Katharine Susannah Prichard grew tired of waiting for an Australian theatre to be born.

iv
The Text

Brumby Innes was published in 1940 by Paterson's Press, Perth. A copy of this first and only edition, at present in the possession of Mr. Ric Throssell, contains manuscript alterations by the author and appears to constitute her final revision of the play. It is therefore followed in this edition.

The alterations to the published text are of minor dramatic consequence except perhaps in Act One, where some reduction and simplification of the corroboree songs helps launch the play more vigorously. Otherwise the alterations seem directed to explicitness: frequent stage directions are inserted to indicate the actors' tone; much of the Aboriginal dialect is recast into a form of English, while the speech of the white men has been altered to indicate accent (going becomes goin', you becomes yer). Horses and a buggy have been written out of the play, presumably in a concession to modernity. The revised text also carries a number of notes on Aboriginal words. Since these and related matters are fully covered in the present volume by Dr. von Brandenstein, it was judged pointless to reprint them. All revisions of the actual text, however, are noted, with the exception of punctuation. A few mis–spellings in the MS. revisions are silently rectified.

Bid Me To Love has never before been published. We give here the text of a typescript in the possession of Mr. Ric Throssell. It is apparently unique.

Katharine Brisbane

BID ME TO LOVE

or

The Caught Bus

Bid Me To Love was first performed by the Canberra Repertory Society at Theatre Three, Canberra, on 10 March 1973, with the following cast:

GREG REED	John Thompson
LOUISE REED	Edith Thompson
MOLLY	Joan Shanahan
JOHN MAINE WOODBRIDGE	Phil Mackenzie
MISS KENNY	Margery Ehnhuus
DON	Julian Owen
BILL	Dan Wilson
PEG	Bethan David
CHILDREN	Michael Wilson
	Michael Shanahan
	Meg Crawford
	Annabelle Shanahan
	Catherine Milne
	Sarah Milne

Setting designed by Bob Warren
Directed by Ric Throssell

John Thompson (Greg) with Bethan David (Peg) and Dan Wilson (Bill) in the Canberra Repertory Society's production of Bid Me To Love. *Photo by Gab Carpay.*

Julian Owen (Don) and Edith Thompson (Louise) in the Canberra Repertory Society's production. Photo by Gab Carpay.

CHARACTERS:

GREG REED LOUISE REED }	six years married
MOLLY	a pretty, up-to-date girl
JOHN MAINE WOODBRIDGE	distinguished author and playwright
MISS KENNY	middle-aged, the local gossip
DON	young, handsome, of Italian extraction
BILL PEG }	the young children of GREG and LOUISE

Several other children, friends of BILL and PEG.

ACT ONE

Verandah of the REEDS' cottage in the hills east of Perth. A sunshiny autumn morning in the late 1920s.

ACT TWO

The REEDS' living room. The following night.

ACT THREE

The verandah. One month later.

ACT ONE

Verandah of the REEDS' *cottage in the hills, at breakfast time on a sunshiny autumn morning.*

There is a railing round the verandah and a prospect of blue hills. A small table with fruit and white cloth, spirit lamp for the coffee pot and silver entrée dishes, stands to the right, not quite centre. There is a gate in the railing lower down the verandah and a door to the house on the left wall at the back. A telephone on the wall inside the door.

GREG, *sitting in tennis flannels at the end of the table, is waiting to begin breakfast, turning the pages of the morning paper.*

GREG: Louise!

LOUISE: [*indoors*] Coming.

> GREG *settles to his paper again.*

GREG: Louise…

> LOUISE, *in kimono and black satin mules, comes on to the verandah from the house as he speaks.*

Oh, there you are, sweetheart.

> *He rises to kiss her as she comes up to him.*

LOUISE: Many happy returns.

GREG: [*holding her*] Cripes, darling, yes. Could anything be better?

> *He looks out to the hills.*

LOUISE: Did you hear the maggies this morning? And that tang in the air, Greg… the smell of apples in the orchard.

GREG: Good, isn't it?

LOUISE: [*sitting*] The sunshine gets into your marrow… But goodness, let's eat… even if we have survived six years of married life with tolerable success.

GREG: [*as they sit*] Tolerable?

LOUISE: [*hearing the ka ka*] A crow…

GREG: Mushrooms, eggs and bacon. [*As* LOUISE *takes an apple*] Aren't you going to have some?

LOUISE: No.

GREG: [*serving himself*] But where did the mushrooms come from?

LOUISE: Don brought them.

GREG: Don, eh! Good old Don! Oh! I wanted to see him. You might ask him to keep an eye out for my yarder. It'll be a bit of a rush going to Sydney tomorrow.

LOUISE: He's in the orchard picking apples.

GREG: Not working at the quarries now?

LOUISE: Been clearing over at Rocky Creek. The place has gone to rack and ruin since his father's death. Don's going to clear and fence, try to make a do of it, he says, and take odd jobs round about, ploughing and picking.

DON *is heard singing 'Bid Me To Love'.*

GREG: There he is now. [*Going to the edge of the verandah and calling*] I say, Don.

DON: [*below in the orchard*] Hullo!

GREG: My yarder's got out of the paddock. You might keep an eye out for him over your way... I'm going to Sydney tomorrow evening... and he'll make back to Mundi... if he gets a chance.

DON: Right.

GREG *goes back to the table.* LOUISE *is pouring coffee.*

LOUISE: I might go after him myself. Haven't been for a ride for ages.

GREG: You don't mean to say you'll ride Joybells?

LOUISE: No, *thank* you. Don can have her. I'll ride his horse. But how is she behaving just now?

GREG: Who?

LOUISE: Joybells.

GREG: Jumping out of her skin; fresh as paint.

LOUISE: [*going behind him and leaning over as she puts down his coffee*] You used to say...

GREG: You're as like as two pins.

LOUISE: [*ruefully*] Fresh...

GREG: But you are the dead ring of her, dearest. She's a thoroughbred if ever there was one: plays up, prances around—all spirit, sweats herself silly over nothing at all. But there's not a spot of vice in her.

DON: [*singing in the distance*] 'And love thee... love thee for ever... and ever.'

GREG: Does he ever sing anything else?

LOUISE: [*laughing*] He's practising for the tennis social and dance.

GREG: Tomorrow night, isn't it? You're going to play for him... I suppose.

LOUISE: Mm. The express goes at eight. I'll see you off first and go down to the hall about nine.

GREG: [*calling over the balcony*] Say, old man... give us the next verse. [*To* LOUISE] These sentimental ballads get my goat. 'Love thee for ever and ever.' Did you ever hear such tommy rot?

LOUISE: [*lightly*] And here was I just thinking you endorsed 'thim sentiments'.

GREG: With you darling, of course. But... a man doesn't run after a caught bus, does he?

LOUISE: [*with surprised indignation*] Greg!

GREG: Wouldn't he be a fool to?

LOUISE: Do you think I'm a caught bus?

GREG: Well, you are, aren't you? [*Engagingly*] Of all the trophies I ever won for running, swimming or boxing, I'm proudest of you, darling. Did it in record time too, didn't I?

LOUISE: You did...

GREG: Cripes. [*With deep feeling*] You're the only woman in the world for me, Louise. We'll have a honeymoon when I get home.

LOUISE: [*after they have kissed, happily*] Dear old thing. That blessed crow!

GREG: Why [*laughing*] I thought you weren't superstitious.

LOUISE: I'm not, but I hate crows... and on a morning... like this...

GREG: My dear, there are millions of crows.

LOUISE: I know, but I hate them. [*Sitting down again and going on with her apple*] Oh well, it seems too good to last.

GREG: What?

LOUISE: Our happiness. I'm afraid even to say that.

GREG: Of course, it will last.

LOUISE: But always when I've felt like this... something has happened. When you say, 'I'm happy', it's as if the Furies were lying in wait to snatch the words away from you and make you suffer for them.

GREG: Oh I say…

MOLLY: [*calling in the garden below*] Hullo there!

LOUISE: Molly.

MOLLY: [*still out of sight*] Greg!

GREG: Cripes, I promised to have a hit with her this morning.

MOLLY: [*a pretty up-to-date girl in tennis turn-out, coming in at the end of the verandah*] Well I'm blest! [*To* JOHN MAINE WOODBRIDGE *behind her*] They haven't finished breakfast yet. [*Advancing*] I've brought an old friend to see you, Mrs. Greg.

LOUISE: [*rising to meet* WOODBRIDGE] John! [*As he bows before her*] Greg, this is my old friend, John Maine Woodbridge, the distinguished author and playwright, re-visiting his native land. Didn't I read that somewhere?

GREG: Heard of you, sir…

WOODBRIDGE: And I of you.

LOUISE: But where on earth have you dropped from, John?

MOLLY: He's staying at the Hills' house.

He goes and sits on the verandah railing.

LOUISE: Talk of an answer to prayer. I've thought so often, 'If Woody could see this.' Knowing just how you'd love the hills, those old gums and…

WOODBRIDGE: It's wonderful, being home again.

GREG: Just back from the Old Dart, are you?

WOODBRIDGE: Arrived by the Naldera on Thursday. First smell of bush fires up here went to my head. Missed the boat back.

LOUISE: Breath of the country, after you've been away so long. Lovely, isn't it?

WOODBRIDGE: I've been drunk with it.

MOLLY: Well, you two can talk flora and fauna, if you like, but how about that game, Greg? I left the girls up on the court cursing you.

GREG: Cripes.

MOLLY: Forget you and I were to play off this morning?

GREG: Forget, Moll? Been dreaming of it all night. [*Slapping his pockets*] Got a cig? I'm not smoking.

MOLLY: [*getting down to hand him her cigarette case; to* LOUISE *and*

WOODBRIDGE] We're playing off for the tournament. [*Going back to the railing*] Where's Don? I hear him somewhere about.

LOUISE: He's picking apples.

MOLLY: [*regretfully*] I wanted him to help me. But he said he'd be too busy ploughing at his place.

GREG: What's the time? Nine. Weren't we to play at nine, Moll? I was never late for anything in my life.

LOUISE: [*as he goes off indoors*] Oh, Greg!

MOLLY: Coming up, Mrs. Greg? It'll be a good go if G's in form. I'm as nervous as a cat, but awfully thrilled at being Greg's partner. [*Seeing* DON *on the path below*] Oh, Don, if you've got a Cleo or a Snow, I'd like it. [*Catching the red apple* DON *tosses up*] Thanks.

> She rubs it and chews, looking after DON over the verandah railing.

WOODBRIDGE: You don't play, Louise?

LOUISE: I'm not a sport of any sort.

MOLLY: Oh, I say.

GREG: [*coming back with racquet and hat*] You don't mind, dear?

LOUISE: No, of course.

MOLLY: Tat-ta, see you again, Mr. Woodbridge.

> They go off through the verandah gate.

WOODBRIDGE: [*sitting on the verandah railing*] It's all very beautiful Louise.

LOUISE: Isn't it?

WOODBRIDGE: Life here has a quality of dreamlike beauty.

LOUISE: It has… this morning.

WOODBRIDGE: Of course, I knew you were somewhere in Australia, but I didn't expect to find you so soon…

LOUISE: And you… to have dropped out of the blue like this, Woody!

WOODBRIDGE: Has life been as good to you as it seems?

LOUISE: It has, I think. There have been storms, of course. But I've got two of the bonniest children you ever saw.

WOODBRIDGE: And… your husband?

LOUISE: We've been married six years today, and he's more in love with me than he ever was, he says.

WOODBRIDGE: And you?

LOUISE: It's true of me, too, I think. We've grown together.

WOODBRIDGE: You've quite got over any old tendernesses?

LOUISE: There's a little flame at the back of my mind, perhaps. But this is different. Living's one thing; loving's another.

WOODBRIDGE: I agree, of course. But…

LOUISE: You didn't expect me to settle into such respectable sobriety?

WOODBRIDGE: Have you?

LOUISE: Don't I look it?

WOODBRIDGE: Not particularly.

LOUISE: You mean this? [*Touching her kimono*] I've done quite a lot of housework, and had my bath. But dress before breakfast I can't. It's one of those old bad habits I don't get out of.

WOODBRIDGE: You're surprised at yourself.

LOUISE: I am. But when we were married, I said to Greg: 'If I don't like it, married life, don't expect me to stick it, will you? And if you don't like it, I won't expect you to stick it, either.'

WOODBRIDGE: Not a point of view he was quite accustomed to, I should think.

LOUISE: Greg has been a very well brought up young man. It was rather a shock to him, but—

WOODBRIDGE: He got used to it.

LOUISE: I believe really, the success of our marriage has been due to… a sense of its impermanence. [*Frowning slightly*] I've said: 'If ever there's anyone you care for more than me, Greg, I'll make way. We'll be good friends. Only tell me.'

WOODBRIDGE: Same old guff.

LOUISE: Woody.

WOODBRIDGE: Well, isn't it?

LOUISE: No, it isn't. Physical fidelity doesn't mean as much to me as psychological fidelity.

WOODBRIDGE: Sex. Damn sex, I say. I'm fed up with it. If only you women would let it fall into its proper place.

LOUISE: I think I do.

WOODBRIDGE: Life and work are more important.

LOUISE: So long as you've disposed of… sex.

WOODBRIDGE: You think you have?

LOUISE: I hope so…

WOODBRIDGE: Every woman believes her husband is the only faithful husband in the world.

LOUISE: Have I any illusions about Greg, I wonder? He adores a tart, has innumerable girl swains; likes to make their hearts flutter, be a thrill to them. But I really think he prides himself more on his fidelity... than I do.

WOODBRIDGE: But all the same, you believe that you have been the only woman for these six years.

LOUISE: It's odd, knowing your adorable sex as I do, isn't it?

WOODBRIDGE: Louise! Louise!

LOUISE: I may be as foolish as every other woman, but really, John, there hasn't been any reason to think anything else. Greg has been the most adoring and devoted lover.

WOODBRIDGE: So have I.

LOUISE: But I've no illusions about you...

WOODBRIDGE: Except one.

LOUISE: One?

WOODBRIDGE: That there are no illusions to have about me.

LOUISE: Oh, and are there?

WOODBRIDGE: At least, I've given you what you say means most to you.

LOUISE: Woody!

WOODBRIDGE: Psychological loyalty. But damn sex: damn it, I say. Dispose of it and let's get on with our work.

LOUISE: By all means.

WOODBRIDGE: If only women could keep a sense of humour in their love affairs.

LOUISE: *Men* do... always?

WOODBRIDGE: You think I lost mine when you married Greg?

LOUISE: You found it again very soon, didn't you Woody? But look, I must clear away. Wash up, do my housework, get lunch.

WOODBRIDGE: What?

LOUISE: Thoroughly domesticated. The genuine article, my dear. Do all my own housework.

WOODBRIDGE: I'm blest.

LOUISE: [*lightly*] A tragedy, isn't it? And you thinking you could write a play here, an Australian play. The successful author and playwright returns to his native heath to write a play about it.

WOODBRIDGE: Well, why not?

LOUISE: A play without a butler and smart maid floating round? My dear Woody, what are you thinking of? Except for their appearance in American and British comedies, these noble creatures are scarcely known among us—except perhaps as vice-regal curiosities.

MISS KENNY: [*calling outside*] Mrs. Greg? Are you there, Mrs. Greg?

LOUISE: And then too, by hook or by crook, if you want any producer to look at your play, you'll have to drag in a French actress—

WOODBRIDGE: Drag her in?

LOUISE: By the heels, if possible—necessary, I mean. A ballet girl, or some bright young thing from the chorus might do. [*As* MISS KENNY *appears, coming from the door into the house*] This is the best I can do for you.

MISS KENNY: [*trotting forward*] Oh, there you are, my dear!

> MISS KENNY *is plump and good-natured, but having gone short of romance in her own life, feasts on it in the lives of others. She is the local gossip. Her skirts are short, she wears gay garters, and a green parrot in her hat leans forward in the perpetual attitude of making a peck at her nose.*

I've been knocking and knocking!

LOUISE: Oh, Miss Kenny, really? I am sorry. Woody, this is my very good neighbour, Miss Kenny. Mr. John Maine Woodbridge, the distinguished author and playwright: Miss Lucretia Kenny.

MISS KENNY: [*tripping forward to shake hands*] Pleased to meet you, Mr. Woodbridge.

WOODBRIDGE: Please to be met—by you, Mrs. Kenny.

MISS KENNY: Miss Kenny.

WOODBRIDGE: I beg your pardon.

MISS KENNY: [*taking* GREG's *chair at the table, confidentially to* LOUISE] I've got it.

LOUISE: Got it?

MISS KENNY: [*nodding her head delightedly*] Yes. I've got it.

LOUISE: But what?

MISS KENNY: The first step. It goes: one, two, together. [*Demonstrating the first step of the Charleston, in the awkward top–heavy fashion of a beginner*] One, two, together; one, two, together.

LOUISE: Oh, Miss Kenny, dear [*as* MISS KENNY *overbalances, nearly topples over and* WOODBRIDGE *goes to her assistance*] do be careful.

MISS KENNY: [*breathless and triumphant*] But that's right, isn't it? Molly said to practise hanging on to a chair. And I did, last night, for nearly an hour.

WOODBRIDGE: Nothing like it. I took to a chair myself.

LOUISE: [*as* MISS KENNY *shuffles laboriously, humming 'Oh, she has naughty eyes, naughty eyes '*] That's it. You've got it, Miss Kenny.

MISS KENNY: [*subsiding into her chair*] Oh-h. And have you heard the news?

LOUISE: No… whatever it is.

MISS KENNY: Mrs. Properjohn, the second [*to* WOODBRIDGE] Molly's stepmother, that is—has twins.

LOUISE: Twins!

MISS KENNY: Boys, both of them, and old Properjohn is beside himself with excitement. By the way, my dear, is it true that Mr. Properjohn and your husband have quarrelled? Seriously, I mean?

LOUISE: Not that I know of.

MISS KENNY: Well, everybody's saying they've had an awful row, and Mr. Properjohn has as good as sacked your husband. Says he is going to close the quarries and Greg is going to Sydney to try and raise money to buy them.

LOUISE: [*laughing*] I wish he were. No. Greg is going to Sydney on business for Mr. Properjohn. And perhaps the quarries will be closed if he doesn't bring it off, but—

MISS KENNY: Molly told me. She said Mr. Reed was going to Sydney to try to raise money to buy the quarries, and most likely she would elope with him and there'd be a divorce and you'd marry Don.

LOUISE: Oh, dear Miss Kenny. [*Laughing*] I'm afraid Molly was pulling your leg. [*To* WOODBRIDGE] You see the way romances are made in a country district.

MISS KENNY: She said… but I thought she didn't mean it. Molly Properjohn is far too much in love with Don herself, if I know anything about it, to think of letting anyone else marry him.

LOUISE: Is she?

MISS KENNY: Only he's so taken up with somebody else, he doesn't even see she's about.

LOUISE: Drama in village gossip. Miss Kenny, you've all the imagination and sense of the theatre these poor old playwrights dream of.

The telephone bell goes.

Hasn't she, Woody?

She goes to answer the telephone at the far end of the verandah, near the door into the house.

MISS KENNY: [*confidentially and a little piqued, to* WOODBRIDGE] All the same... Don thinks the sun shines—

LOUISE: [*at the telephone*] Yes. One hundred and one, West Range.

MISS KENNY: ...out of her.

LOUISE: Who? Mr. Reed is out. A wire?

WOODBRIDGE: He does, does he?

LOUISE: Oh, well, you'd better give it to me. He's leaving for Sydney tomorrow and won't be in the office again.

MISS KENNY: Mind, I don't say there's anything in it—

LOUISE: Will you please repeat the message? Where's that pencil? [*Writing*] I'll see Mr. Reed gets it as soon as he comes in. Thank you, Fred.

She puts down the receiver and stands gazing before her.

WOODBRIDGE: What is it? Not bad news, I hope, Louise?

LOUISE: [*startled out of her preoccupation, coming forward*] No. At least...

WOODBRIDGE: My dear?

LOUISE: It's not bad news, Woody. Really. [*Trying to talk lightly*] A shock, rather. A message for Greg. They phoned it through from the office.

WOODBRIDGE: Is it urgent? Shall I take it up to the tennis court?

LOUISE: No. I think it can wait, thank you. [*As* MISS KENNY *rises to go*] You're not going, Miss Kenny? About tomorrow night...

MISS KENNY: Don told me you wanted to see me.

LOUISE: Greg goes to Sydney by the evening train and I've promised to play for Don at the tennis social and dance. [*To* WOODBRIDGE] Miss Kenny is a very good kind neighbour who stays with the children sometimes when I want to go out. Could you come in tomorrow night, Miss Kenny?

MISS KENNY: Of course I'll come, my dear. I want to alter my hat. It'll just fit in nicely. Poor Polly is beginning to moult.

LOUISE: Is she?

MISS KENNY: [*taking off her hat and showing it to* WOODBRIDGE] You see, I've worn her for—let me see—how many winters, is it, my dear?

LOUISE: It must be three or four, at least.

MISS KENNY: You see, she was my pet, my very pettest pet, and when she died I felt so lonely. I had her stuffed—and I've worn her in my hat ever since. Now her feathers are coming out...

LOUISE: It's quite time she had a decent burial.

MISS KENNY: Yes. I think so.

WOODBRIDGE: Quite. Oh, quite.

MISS KENNY: Don promised to dig a grave for me in the garden... and they say flowers are going to be fashionable this spring. I've bought a wreath of roses and forget-me-nots to go in her place.

WOODBRIDGE: Appropriate. Very appropriate!

MISS KENNY: Isn't it roses for love? And forget-me-nots? Polly'd be pleased, wouldn't she, if she knew? [*Putting on her hat and moving off with a little shuffle*] Oh, and dearie, you won't forget to leave a book for me, will you? Something pink...

> BILL *is heard calling as she trots off, Charlestoning, 'one, two, together...'.*

BILL: Mummy! Mummy!

> DON *comes through the wicket gate onto the verandah with the children.* BILL *is a sturdy boy of about five and* PEG *perhaps a year younger.* DON, *a good-looking young man of Italian extraction, but Australian in every word and gesture, wears well-washed blue dungarees with an apple bag slung round his neck.* MISS KENNY *hesitates when she sees him just as she is going out.*

DON: Hullo, Miss Kenny!

MISS KENNY: Oh, Don...

> *She goes out.*

BILL: [*running to* LOUISE] Mummy. Don's got the beautifulest moth for you.

LOUISE: Has he, darling? See, this is an old friend of Mummie's.

John Maine Woodbridge, the distinguished author and playwright, revisiting his native land. John: my son, Bill.

> BILL *stands with his hand on his tummy and makes a funny formal little bow.*

WOODBRIDGE: Billy.

LOUISE: And this is Peg. Go and say how-do-you-do to Mr. Woodbridge, darling.

> *The child clings to her mother.*

And Don. Mr. Rudolf Giacomo Lorenze Donatello.

> DON *swings the apple bag from his shoulder.*

Called Bob for short—the Don by this family—and Don, because he likes it better.

DON: [*with easy indifference*] How do y'do?

> *He hands a cigarette box containing the moth to* LOUISE.

LOUISE: The moth! [*Opening the box*] Oh, Don, what a beauty.

DON: He was asleep on the tree.

BILL: Let me see. Let me see, Mum!

WOODBRIDGE: [*looking into the box*] By Jove, what a splendid chap.

LOUISE: Do you know him, Don?

DON: No, he's rare about here. A stranger. I've never seen him before.

LOUISE: Bill darling! Oh, do be careful.

WOODBRIDGE: A bombycidae, if I'm not mistaken.

DON: [*to* LOUISE] Thought you'd like him.

> *Picking up the apple bag, he turns to go.*

LOUISE: Didn't think you knew anything about moths, Woody.

WOODBRIDGE: I don't—much. A little imagination goes a long way. I was speaking of [*with a movement of his head towards* DON's *back*] the Don, rather.

GREG: [*coming in the verandah gate*] They want some balls. [*Passing* DON *on his way out*] Oh, I say, Don, you won't forget about Yarraman? He'll probably make up your way to the creek.

DON: I won't forget.

GREG: And I say, do you think you could drive me over to the station tomorrow evening? I'll put Joybells in the sulky.

DON: Right.

GREG: Better leave at about eight, I suppose. Was never late for anything in my life. Oh, and I say, Don, got a cigarette? I'm not smoking. [*As* DON *holds out a packet*] Thanks, thanks awfully old chap.

> DON *goes out by the verandah gate.*

Powerful fellow, eh? Good-looker?

WOODBRIDGE: Rather.

LOUISE: [*calling after him*] Don! [*As he appears at the end of the verandah again*] Those crows. What on earth are they doing? I do hate crows.

DON: I'll have a bang at them.

LOUISE: Will you?

> DON *disappears again.*

BILLY: Mummie's got the beautifulest moth, Daddy. Don bringed her.

GREG: Did he?

LOUISE: Look. [*Showing the moth in its box*] Here he is.

GREG: Oh, I say, isn't he a beauty? [*To* WOODBRIDGE] These chaps about here, fellers and sleeper cutters, think Louise is Christmas. Bring her all sorts of moths and grubs. And if there's an accident in the quarries, a man cuts his finger or has a bingee ache—

LOUISE: Greg!

WOODBRIDGE: How's the tennis?

GREG: [*picking up one of the apples which has rolled from* DON'*s bag, and chewing*] We haven't played yet. Been put off until this afternoon. But we'll beat 'em all right. Molly's got a slashing serve. We won our two rounds yesterday without turning a hair. Of course Kath Brown plays a rattling good game: there's no two ways about it. But Dick drops his bundle if he doesn't win at once. Staying to lunch?

LOUISE: He's not asked.

WOODBRIDGE: [*ready to go*] Oh, I say, mayn't I stay?

GREG: Might not be any lunch by the look of things.

LOUISE: Tomorrow night, Woody, will you come and have dinner with us? Then you can cheer me up when Greg has gone.

GREG: But aren't you playing for Don at the social and dance?

LOUISE: Woody can come too.

WOODBRIDGE: Delighted, of course.

> *As he turns to go,* GREG *precedes him to open the verandah gate and follows him out.* LOUISE *packs dishes from the table to a tray.*

GREG: [*coming back*] Too bad of me to clear off.

LOUISE: Oh, I did nearly everything before breakfast, this morning.

GREG: I'll give you a hand now. [*Gathering up knives and spoons*] By the way, though… you never told me John Maine Woodbridge was a friend of yours?

LOUISE: [*slowly*] Didn't I? I think… I did.

GREG: A great friend too; nicknames and all of that. [*Somewhat aggrieved*] Cripes, Louise—

LOUISE: Talking of nicknames, there's a message for you. A wire. Came while you were at the court and Fred rang it through from the office.

GREG: [*as she goes off with the tray*] Where is it?

LOUISE: On the table, there.

> *She goes out.*

GREG: [*reading*] Meeting Sydney as arranged. Joybells. Well—I'm damned.

> LOUISE *returns to the table again and fills her tray.*

It's from… Joybells.

LOUISE: Another of your little thoroughbreds?

GREG: But I say, Louise: you're not taking this seriously?

LOUISE: [*turning away as he bends forward to kiss her, and going out with the tray*] That crow seems to have known what he was talking about!

END OF ACT ONE

ACT TWO

The following evening. Living room of the REEDS' *home—a beautiful room in the colours of black opal, with French doors open along the back, showing blue night sky. Over a bookcase, to the left of the doors, there is a mirror. A table, the disorder of a meal still on it, straddles the front, on the left; a servery cupboard in the wall behind it. Further along on the left, a piano and door. A big comfortable lounge is crosswise on the right; the door to the bedrooms is nearer the front on the right.*

LOUISE, *at the piano, plays a few bars of 'Bid Me To Love' absent-mindedly, then rises and moves away impatiently.* WOODBRIDGE, *who has been standing by, holds his cigarette case out to her.*

WOODBRIDGE: Well?

LOUISE: [*taking a cigarette*] Greg goes by the express tonight.

> WOODBRIDGE *lights her cigarette,* MOLLY *comes through the French doors, followed by* GREG. *He is dressed for his journey and she has a silk shawl over her dance frock.*

MOLLY: Louise! You're not going to be late for the dance, are you? Greg says Don is coming for him at eight.

LOUISE: I'll see Greg off first.

MOLLY: Oh, well, Mr. Woodbridge, will you drive me down to the hall? And I'll tell Miss Kenny I've changed my mind and decided to elope with you and not Greg.

WOODBRIDGE: With pleasure.

MOLLY: [*tip-toeing to kiss* GREG] Goodbye, old dear. Dad's a mean beast to send you to try and get money out of Paul Adamson. He couldn't do it himself. Now if you'd only take me with you—Ssh, was that Miss Kenny!

GREG: Well, how about it? It's not too late—

MOLLY: I can twist old Adamson round my little finger. Any girl, who knows how, could.

LOUISE: What you'd call... appealing to the mature imagination, Woody?

GREG: [*sulkily*] Mature devils!

WOODBRIDGE: Same thing, aren't they?

MOLLY: [*as they go out, wistfully*] Tell Don I'll keep the extras after supper—for him.

WOODBRIDGE: I'll come back for you, Louise.

LOUISE: Oh, thank you, Woody.

GREG: Don will drive you over, Louise, when he gets back from the station.

LOUISE: No. If you don't mind, Woody. Don can take Joybells out when he gets back and we'll both drive over to the hall with you. She's really much too lively at night.

WOODBRIDGE: Good. [*Going out*] Goodnight and all the luck, Reed.

GREG: You persist in treating this thing seriously, Louise?

LOUISE: It is serious.

GREG: Oh, very well if you want to make tragedy of it—

LOUISE: Listen, Greg. I'm trying not to make tragedy of it. I'm trying to do what I always said I'd do if anything like this cropped up. But—

GREG: Come on, let's have it all again.

LOUISE: It's not necessary, if you'd rather not.

GREG: [*going to her and taking her in his arms, although she holds herself away*] God Almighty, girl. You know I love you. You know you're the only woman in the world for me.

LOUISE: I thought so.

GREG: I've been a fool; a damned fool.

LOUISE: To be found out?

GREG: No. [*Desperately*] Yes… well, yes, I suppose that's it.

LOUISE: Is it impossible really for any man to be honest with his wife? I believe Celia was right after all. A school-fellow of mine who joined what you call 'the oldest profession in the world'. *Très chic* and charming. 'There's only one way with men, darling,' she said. 'Emulate the spider. Take the b——'s when you want them; but don't let them interfere with your life at all.'

GREG: Louise! I can't bear to hear you talk like that—

LOUISE: I thought we understood each other so well: if ever another woman came into your life—

GREG: Come into my life? Haven't I told you I've never even met this woman.

LOUISE: Only written her love letters and arranged to 'warm her soul case for her' next week in Sydney.

GREG: Oh well, damn it all—

LOUISE: I don't want to make the usual scene. I want to say—as I always said I would: 'Right, old dear. Go ahead.'

GREG: Oh well, damn it all, Louise.

LOUISE: And I do say that. Only… it's not quite as easy as I thought it would be.

GREG: Don's putting the pony in, now. We've only a few minutes. If so much didn't depend on my doing this job, I wouldn't go tonight. I can't leave you like this.

LOUISE: But you will.

GREG: You know I've got to go, or throw up my job.

LOUISE: You must go. And I want you to succeed in whatever you set out to do, Greg. That's why—

GREG: I promise you I won't see the blasted woman.

LOUISE: That wouldn't do. You see, I've got to keep faith with myself. I've got to let you be free to do… what you want to do. There's only one condition: you've got to tell me—

GREG: Hell.

LOUISE: Not that I'll believe… what you say. [*As he moves impatiently*] It's not fair to expect me to, is it?

GREG: Expect? Expect? God knows what I expect you to do—except that you won't do it.

LOUISE: Greg?

GREG: Well, you know you never do what anybody expects you to, Louise.

LOUISE: Would you rather I'd do what everybody expects me to?

GREG: Of course. At least—Oh damn!

DON: [*calling outside*] Hullo there! Are you ready, Mr. Reed?

GREG: There's Don.

LOUISE: What everybody'd expect me to do would be to make a scene, pack up and—forgive you.

GREG: And you're not making a scene?

LOUISE: Am I?

GREG: Merely discussing the situation in a spirit of sweet reasonableness.

LOUISE: You'd rather I raved and wept?

GREG: [*passionately*] Anything. Anything so long as you wiped the whole thing out.

LOUISE: It's not a bit of good talking like that, Greg. We've got to try ourselves out on this; face it and try to discover what we do really want. I've told you I'll stand by. The household will go on as usual. I'll be your best friend, until—

GREG: Louise!

LOUISE: Only... I won't live with treachery.

GREG: I say, draw it mild.

LOUISE: It's too ugly. I won't have my mind poisoned as it has been since yesterday. I won't be jealous.

GREG: [*maliciously*] But you are.

LOUISE: Yes, perhaps. But I hate it. I won't let myself be. I won't grudge you anything you want, Greg. That's why—

GREG: Aren't we making ourselves desperately miserable about nothing at all? I've told you I love you. You're the only woman in the world for me.

LOUISE: Does she think so?

GREG: Damn. The fact of the matter is you don't love me. You never have loved me.

LOUISE: I don't like you at present, I don't like what you've done to me.

GREG: God Almighty, what have I done? After all what have I done?

LOUISE: You've given my name to another woman. You've called another woman your little thoroughbred. And but for an accident, you'd be warming her soul case for her in Sydney, on this day week.

DON: [*calling outside*] I say there—

GREG: Right Don! [*Going to the door*] Would you put in that suitcase? [*Crossing to the bedroom and returning with a smaller case, hat and rug*] Well, you won't kiss and be friends?

LOUISE: [*pacifically*] Friends, of course. Have you got everything? Rug, books?

DON: [*coming in, sharply*] We'll just about do it.

He goes out again.

GREG: [*getting into his coat and hat*] It's all right, Don. Was never late for anything in my life. [*Grabbing* LOUISE *and giving her a hug*] You'll see, when I get back I'll make you forget—

LOUISE: There. [*Tucking a muffler round his throat*] It'll be cold in the train. [*As* DON *is heard calling*] Coming, Don! [*Kissing him lightly*] I'll kiss the kiddies for you. And don't forget you're to be as free as air in Sydney.

GREG: Free devils!

He goes out and, rushing back, seizes her.

You've got to say you care. Or I'll blow me light out, see. Say it. Say it!

LOUISE: Greg... for goodness sake... You'll miss—

GREG: Say you love me, then.

LOUISE: Love you. [*Mockingly*] Like hell. But—

GREG: What?

He dashes out.

LOUISE: [*after he has gone*] I won't forgive you till you've got something to forgive me.

She goes to the French doors and leans against them, looking out. A yellow cat hops on to the table behind her. She sighs, and, hearing the cat, turns.

Oh, Phoebus Apollo!

She chases the cat from the table and, taking a floral apron from the servery cupboard, ties it over her evening dress, and moves the debris of the meal into the servery cupboard.

There are always dishes to wash. Not that I'm going to wash dishes tonight, my Phoebus, just pile them up for the morning. But if you go near the kitchen—Ssh, what was that? The express... [*Going to the window*] Yes, there she goes down to the station. Will they catch her, Phoebus, I wonder? And what goes with her?

BILL: [*stumbling in from the door to the bedrooms with tossed hair and sleepy eyes*] Mummy! Mummy!

LOUISE: Darlingest! What ever is it?

BILL: [*sobbing*] I had a horrible dream.

LOUISE: [*taking him in her arms and sitting down on the lounge*] Darling—

BILL: I dreamed we were in an aeroplane... and... and it magicked everybody to bits. Then it bumped against a cloud... and fell down… and smashed… and there were tigers and lions all round, roaring and roaring—

LOUISE: Precious… But it was only a dream, wasn't it?

BILL: [*looking about him*] Yes.

LOUISE: It's our own room; and there's Phoebus. [*Calling*] Is that you, Woody?

WOODBRIDGE: [*coming in by the door on the left*] It is.

LOUISE: And here's Mummy's old friend, John Maine Woodbridge, the distinguished-author-and-playwright-revisiting-his-native-land. Do you remember, old man?

BILL: [*doubtfully*] Mmm.

LOUISE: He's been having the horridest dream, Woody. You tell Woody about the dream, darling, while I put these things away.

> *She rises to go to the table.*

WOODBRIDGE: By Jove, yes, eh? You tell me about it, Bill.

LOUISE: [*to avert trouble as the child edges away from* WOODBRIDGE] Oh well, I'll tell you what, Bill, we'll make him clear away, shall we? [*Taking off her apron, and tying it round* WOODBRIDGE] That'll teach him, the distinguished author and playwright, to write plays with butlers and maids floating round all the time.

WOODBRIDGE: [*looking helpless and absurd*] Oh, I say—

LOUISE: While I tuck Bill in his beddy-bye.

WOODBRIDGE: [*stacking plates recklessly*] This the way you do it, Bill?

LOUISE: [*taking an apple from the table*] And here's a rosy apple to put under your pillow, for the morning. One for Peg, too.

BILL: And one for Phoebus Apollo?

LOUISE: Yes, one for Phoebus Apollo.

> *They go out by the door to the bedrooms on the right, the child hugging his cat.* WOODBRIDGE *goes on in methodical bachelor fashion putting dishes from the table into the servery, chews a cheese straw, relights the spirit lamp under the coffee pot, takes a cigarette from his case.* LOUISE *comes back, goes to the French doors and looks out.*

I wonder if Greg caught the train?

WOODBRIDGE: I've hotted the coffee. Won't you have a cup?

LOUISE: [*returning to the lounge, sinking down*] Thank you, Woody.

He brings her the coffee, pulls a chair up and, taking the cup from her, puts it down on the chair. He offers his cigarette case. LOUISE *takes a cigarette; he lights it and stands off, smiling at her abstraction.*

WOODBRIDGE: Yesterday, my dear, you were lotus eating. And today you're at anchor in the doldrums.

LOUISE: That's just how I feel. [*Restlessly*] And yet... I don't know how I feel. [*Jumping up restlessly and walking to the French doors, pulling a curtain*] It didn't seem fair to tell you, yesterday, until I heard what Greg had to say. But now... I will. [*Sitting down again*] You remember that telephone message I took while you were here yesterday?

WOODBRIDGE: It gave you something to think about.

LOUISE: [*sipping her coffee*] It was a wire from a woman in Queensland to say she'd meet Greg in Sydney.

WOODBRIDGE: Well?

LOUISE: I cut up rusty about it. I didn't mean... didn't want to.

WOODBRIDGE: What did you want to do?

LOUISE: Oh, I did it, in the end; said to him: 'Right. Go ahead, old dear!' You see, I've never attached much importance to physical fidelity in marriage...

WOODBRIDGE: Why should you?

LOUISE: But Greg has.

WOODBRIDGE: Naturally.

LOUISE: Any man could say that.

WOODBRIDGE: Am I not to say what any man would?

LOUISE: But you know you don't think it. You agree with me.

WOODBRIDGE: I was seeing the thing from your husband's angle.

LOUISE: That's just it. I've been seeing the thing from his angle and lost my own. I thought when we were married, the only way to retain any glamour was for each of us to feel free—free to do what we wished. Greg and I were to tell each other, if... either of us, caught fire again... wandered in our affections...

WOODBRIDGE: He forgot that part of the bargain. Did you ever?

LOUISE: I wish I had.

WOODBRIDGE: He's taken it for granted you're all he thinks you are?

LOUISE: I have been. That's the worst of it. I've been so busy trying to be a good mother and model housewife. There hasn't been time or energy for diversions of any sort.

WOODBRIDGE: Louise, my dear, it's hurt you—

LOUISE: Oh yes, it's hurt, Woody! But the gilt is off the gingerbread. I'm not going to be the caught bus Greg thinks I am.

WOODBRIDGE: You couldn't be a caught bus if you tried.

LOUISE: I couldn't, really. But Greg doesn't suspect it.

WOODBRIDGE: You're too—sex sensitive, my dear.

LOUISE: There are times when… almost any man… who wanted… How shocked Greg would be if he knew. And if I left him—

WOODBRIDGE: You couldn't get past me.

LOUISE: It's damnable, Woody, to have put on the brakes so, and then—

WOODBRIDGE: Don't.

LOUISE: Greg says he suffers from an 'inferiority complex' with me.

WOODBRIDGE: That's why the adoration of the fair unknown appealed to him.

LOUISE: Well, I refuse to suffer from a superiority complex. There's nothing on earth makes me feel so mean and small as forgiving. I hate forgiving. I won't forgive Greg… until I've given him something to forgive me.

WOODBRIDGE: That's it—the Pirandello stuff.

LOUISE: The worst of it is… you don't get any younger.

WOODBRIDGE: [*ruefully*] I? No, I suppose I don't.

LOUISE: Not you. I mean me, Woody. I don't. [*Going over to a mirror on the wall near the French doors*] Not so young and charming as I was.

WOODBRIDGE: [*gallantly*] You're always the most wonderful and beautiful woman in the world, Louise.

LOUISE: Woody! [*Turning from the mirror*] It's nice to hear you say so … again. But I think Greg's right: [*Looking into the mirror again*] 'You're no longer an oil painting, old dear,' he says. See, there's grey in my hair—

WOODBRIDGE: And dye so cheap?

LOUISE: Not so cheap as men.

WOODBRIDGE: Louise!

LOUISE: Well [*laughing, her charm beginning to exert itself*] I don't have to dye my hair to find a lover.

WOODBRIDGE: I'd love you if your hair was green.

LOUISE: And Greg thinks I'm a caught bus. It's quite safe for him to carry on because I've forgotten how.

WOODBRIDGE: Let's learn him.

LOUISE: I'd love to. But not with you, Woody.

WOODBRIDGE: Why not with me? Aren't I eminently suited to... practise... the gentle art?

LOUISE: Perhaps that's why. Besides, I want to know, myself, whether... And you're somehow—

WOODBRIDGE: Taken for granted?

LOUISE: Mmm.

WOODBRIDGE: Greg doesn't think I count, either?

LOUISE: I'm not so sure of that. But, really [*playing the charmer*] it's because you're too dangerous—

WOODBRIDGE: [*breathlessly*] Louise!

LOUISE: [*gaily*] Oh, I can do it still, after all.

WOODBRIDGE: [*chagrined*] I didn't doubt it.

LOUISE: You see ... I seem to have had lovers as long as I can remember ... some small boy or other dancing attendance on me. But lately... lately. [*Desperately*] There's been no time to be elusive and charming.

WOODBRIDGE: You've been overwhelmed by the domesticities.

LOUISE: [*nodding*] And last night, my heart was 'a forsaken bird's nest filled with snow'. Who said that? One of the Irish poets. And then to discover, there's no one, any longer, I 'magic to bits', as Bill says—

WOODBRIDGE: No one?

LOUISE: You. Oh, well... you're the same old darling. You don't count, Woody. But I don't go to your head, even as I used to.

WOODBRIDGE: Don't you?

LOUISE: It doesn't agree with me. Every woman of forty needs a lover to keep her self-respect... and her husband's.

WOODBRIDGE: I'd prescribe one.

LOUISE: It makes you feel young and gay and charming to know you're just Christmas to somebody. That's what Greg—What was it Greg said? You're just Christmas to...?

WOODBRIDGE: Fidelity was never one of your defects, my dear.

LOUISE: [*delightedly, emerging from a thoughtfulness*] I won't be a caught bus, Woody! I won't. I'd make love to a blind man on a dark road to get even with Greg for saying that. But I'm not going to leave him. Marriage, the most serious part of it, is a contract to trot in double harness. There are undertakings in common. The children —I won't have their lives messed up. But I'm going to give Greg something to forgive me—and then we'd cry quits, perhaps—

WOODBRIDGE: My dear—

LOUISE: Not you, Woody dear—though it might quite easily be.

WOODBRIDGE: Louise!

LOUISE: It's perfectly heavenly to have you making love to me again. Have anybody making love to me, Woody! The worst of being married is, you get so involved in the business of living together— meals, drains, mending, and bills—there's nothing left over for subtle philandering. When a lover asks you to dine with him, it is an adventure, a delightful episode held against all others; when your husband asks you to dine with him it's an accident, and he'll tell you what the food cost.

WOODBRIDGE: Come... and let's smell the lemon blossom in the garden.

LOUISE: No.

WOODBRIDGE: [*passionately*] Louise!

He moves to embrace her.

LOUISE: I can't. [*Eluding hint*] Miss Kenny is coming presently to stay with the children while we go to the social. You've never met a social, perhaps...

WOODBRIDGE: My dear, wasn't I raised in a country town? Miss So So recites and Mr. Jones gives a few conjuring tricks.

LOUISE: I've promised to play for Don. By the way, he's the young man I'm thinking of leading astray.

WOODBRIDGE: You're thinking of leading astray?

LOUISE: We're going after that horse, tomorrow. We'll ride through the bush to Rocky Creek. Don's at his best in the bush.

WOODBRIDGE: You won't do anything of the kind.

LOUISE: But I will.

WOODBRIDGE: I won't permit it.

LOUISE: Permit it, Woody?

WOODBRIDGE: Permit it. It's one thing for me to propose a perfectly… well, orthodox… indiscretion with an old love; and another for you to commit yourself to the tempestuous passions of this young Dago.

LOUISE: And if I tell you I am… *passionnée* for this young Dago? Though he isn't Dago at all really, only grandson of an Italian who had vineyards here—

WOODBRIDGE: *Passionnée* be damned. Don't let's lose our sense of humour, Louise.

LOUISE: Sense of humour? Of course, I forgot. Humour in the sex relation is your strong point, isn't it?

WOODBRIDGE: It's not yours, evidently, or you wouldn't be upsetting this young man's apple-cart—

LOUISE: But it's upset, Woody. It really is. I'm only going to help him to pick up a few of the apples.

WOODBRIDGE: Apples be damned.

LOUISE: 'Comfort me with apples for I am sick of love.'

WOODBRIDGE: It's not fair, Louise. A perfectly decent young working man—to turn his head with your airs and graces.

LOUISE: But, really, Woody. Out there, in the forest, when we're riding together, it's the other way about. He's so at home. And like that moth, wild and shy, with beautiful irises on his wings. And I'm… just any female that's happened his way—

WOODBRIDGE: That's all very well, but—

LOUISE: Do you think I… vamp Don? Snake up to him like the wicked lady of the pictures? Talk at his nose [*imitating the movie stunt*] like this? No. [*Laughing*] I don't have to be any sort of siren to Don. That's the best of it. I don't have to dress up for him, even as much as for Greg. Out there in the bush he just sings… and does everything for me. Makes the fire, boils the billy. I feel as happy and carefree as a kid, leaving all this behind… for a day.

WOODBRIDGE: For a day?

LOUISE: I adore his vigour and youthful beauty.

WOODBRIDGE: God, woman—

LOUISE: He really is a very worthy, gentle knight.

WOODBRIDGE: Well, if you go out with him while I'm here—

LOUISE: You're not forgetting, are you, my dear… your humour in the sex relation?

WOODBRIDGE: This isn't funny, Louise.

LOUISE: Isn't it? I see your point, Woody. I've always been afraid I might smash up over some Dionysus, like Don...

WOODBRIDGE: You're quite capable of it. That's why—

LOUISE: That's why I'd rather it were Don... than anyone else.

WOODBRIDGE: I won't permit... I mean... I simply won't stand by and see you make a mess of your life, Louise.

LOUISE: It's awfully sweet of you, Woody. But I don't quite see what you can do.

WOODBRIDGE: Do? I'll write for your husband.

LOUISE: Being a dramatist, I suppose—

WOODBRIDGE: Well, it's pistols for two if you go with him while I'm here.

DON: [*at the door, hat in hand, evening dress under his coat*] May I come in?

LOUISE: Yes, come in, Don. You caught the train?

DON: By the skin of our teeth. The station-master heard us coming and held up the train.

LOUISE: Are your ears burning? We've been talking of you. My old friend, John Maine Woodbridge says if I go for a ride with you, tomorrow, there'll be pistols for two.

      MISS KENNY *comes in by the French doors.*

DON: [*good-humouredly*] I've only got the old crow-banger. How about it?

LOUISE: I'll go, of course.

MISS KENNY: [*rushing forward distractedly*] Oh, my God, what is it? What's the matter?

LOUISE: Oh, Miss Kenny. We're rehearsing a little comedy Mr. Woodbridge has devised. Will you put your things in my room?

      MISS KENNY *crosses to the door on the right, watching carefully, with sidelong glances.*

Oh, and would you bring my cloak from the wardrobe?

MISS KENNY: The velvet one with fur?

LOUISE: Yes, please. [*Glancing at her wrist watch*] Dear, it's late! You want to try over that song, Don, don't you?

She goes to the piano and rummages with the music.

DON: [*taking the song in his hand*] It's here… I don't quite catch on to the accompaniment. [*To* WOODBRIDGE] You see, I'm not used to singing to an accompaniment. Mostly I just shout to myself out in the bush.

LOUISE *plays and he sings 'Bid Me To Love'.* MISS KENNY, *bringing in the cloak, stands to watch and listen.*

LOUISE: Bravo, Don. He has a good voice, hasn't he, Woody?

WOODBRIDGE: [*absent-mindedly*] Quite!

LOUISE: [*as* MISS KENNY *gives her the cloak*] Thank you, Miss Kenny. I've left you a little story called *The Scarlet Sin*. Do you think it'll be pink enough?… If Bill wakes, tell him I'll be back presently, and have a look, won't you, to see Peg doesn't throw off her blanket?

MISS KENNY: Of course, my dear. [*Charlestoning delightedly*] See, I'm getting it, aren't I?

LOUISE: [*laughing*] Yes… that's it!

DON *picks up the handkerchief she lets fall.*

Thank you, Don. I'm afraid we'll be dreadfully late. Coming, Woody? [*Turning mischievously, as they are at the door*] You won't tell anyone, will you, Miss Kenny? But I am so worried. Which of them will I make love to while Greg's away? Don who is young and beautiful, or John Maine Woodbridge… the very nicest of my old sweethearts?

MISS KENNY: Oh!

END OF ACT TWO

ACT THREE

A month later. The verandah, as in ACT ONE. It is early evening. There are Chinese lanterns along the verandah, and at the end, near the gate, a long table is decked for a children's party. Coloured paper streamers have been strung across the roof; a cake glitters with candles; the children are pulling crackers and have donned gaudy paper caps. They have just finished their meal, MOLLY and MISS KENNY presiding, and are singing 'Good Evening to You'. The curtain rises to a gay clamour of children's voices.

BILL: Miss Kenny, may I have some more cake?

PEG: I want birfday cake.

MOLLY: Cake? Cake? Who's for cake?

CHILDREN: Me! Me! Me, please.

PEG: Me wants some cake, please.

BILL: And some pink lolly!

PEG: Can't I have pink lolly too, Bill?

BILL: No… I want the pink lolly and the ship!

PEG: But I want the pink lolly…

BILL: It's my birfday… and my cake!

WOODBRIDGE: [*coming on to the verandah through the gate*] Hullo, everybody!

BILL: It's my birfday, Mr. Woodbridge… I'm five years old, and…

WOODBRIDGE: Five years old! Happy turns, old man.

BILL: [*proudly doing the honours*] And this is Jack and that's Margot and Bobby… and Bet, and this [*with an effort to remember*] is my old friend John Maine Woodbridge, the 'stinguished author and playwright revisiting…

WOODBRIDGE: I say, old man. [*Giving him a small package*] Here's a little parcel for you… but you have to give me a ha'penny so as not to cut friendship. And may I have a piece of cake?

BILL: [*busy unfolding his parcel*] May he have a piece of cake, Miss Kenny?

MISS KENNY: [*passing a plate with cake on it*] Of course.

BILL: [*taking the plate and passing it on*] There. It's a big bit and there's a lolly on it.

WOODBRIDGE: A lolly! I am in luck, aren't I?

MISS KENNY: I'm awfully worried, Mr. Woodbridge.

WOODBRIDGE: Mrs. Reed not back yet?

MISS KENNY:She rode over to Mardourie with Don for the show, yesterday. Was to have been back early this morning—and she's not, yet.

WOODBRIDGE: But—

MISS KENNY: The others are back. They motored, of course, but Molly says—

MOLLY: Mrs. Greg and Don left when we did… but they took the bush track.

WOODBRIDGE: I see.

MOLLY: She'd never have been late for this—

MISS KENNY: If she could help it.

WOODBRIDGE: Bill's birthday. No, I suppose not.

MOLLY: [*while the children crowd round* BILL, *examining the knife or pulling crackers*] She'd have rung up from somewhere.

BILL: Look… look… three blades… an' a corkscrew. And what's that, Jack?

MISS KENNY: There's been an accident or something. And the worst of it is…

WOODBRIDGE: Yes?

MISS KENNY: A wire came from Mr. Reed, just after she had gone, to say… he'd be home tonight.

WOODBRIDGE: She was riding Yarraman?

MOLLY: Yes.

WOODBRIDGE: I'll take the mare, then.

MOLLY: You couldn't get her tonight. She's in the big paddock, hasn't been ridden since Greg left.

WOODBRIDGE: I'll get a horse from the Hills' then. Where do I strike the track through the bush—Mardourie track?

MOLLY: Listen…

MISS KENNY: It's Don singing.

DON: [*in the distance, faint and very far away*] 'I do not ask to be this unto thee, but love thee… love thee for ever and ever.'

MISS MOLLY: [*going to the gate to listen*] She's singing, too.

KENNY: It's all right, then. Thank goodness.

WOODBRIDGE: What time does the train get in?

MOLLY: Eight o'clock. It's ten to, now.

> LOUISE *enters by the verandah gate, wearing riding pants, brown corduroy velvet jacket and wide hat of brown velour, a sprig of wattle blossom in her hat band.*

LOUISE: Billy! Billikins! My little William bird.

BILL: Mummy!

> *He runs to her. She catches him to her and pulls out one of the chairs beside the table.*

LOUISE: Did you think Mum had forgotten your birthday, darling? It was all that old Yarraman's fault. Nearly jumped out of his skin at a bit of moonlight; and Don's been half the night chasing him. See what I've got in my pocket for you...

BILL: [*diving into a pocket of her coat and pulling out a banksia cone*] A banksia man. Oh Mum!

LOUISE: I found it—and Don made it. Hullo, Woody! Oh, Miss Kenny, you are a dear to look after the children like this for me. And you, Moll. [*Sitting down and going on with her story to* BILL] And there was me, darling, sitting up against a tree, trying to be brave—and a bit hurted. [*As* DON *comes through the verandah gate*] There you are, Don. Do come and have something to eat. I'm starved myself.

MOLLY: [*when* DON *does not appear to have noticed her*] Don!

DON: [*carelessly*] Oh, hullo, Moll!

WOODBRIDGE: [*curtly*] Good evening.

DON: Good evening.

LOUISE: Have the children left anything to eat, Miss Kenny?

MISS KENNY: There's a bit of chookie in the safe, I think.

> *She trots off indoors to get it.*

LOUISE: [*to the children*] Shoo, darlings! You go and play blind man's buff in the garden till we've had some tucker.

MOLLY: I'll take them. [*Going out the verandah gate*] Come along kiddies!

> *The children romp out after her.*

LOUISE: You've... dined, I suppose, Woody?

WOODBRIDGE: Thank you.

LOUISE: Well, you could play butler—if you don't mind. Bring me some wine. And a biscuit, if there is one.

WOODBRIDGE: Right.

He goes out into the house. When he has gone, LOUISE *puts her hand on* DON's *arm, with tender familiarity.*

LOUISE: Don!

DON: I'd rather go. Let me go, now. I can't bear it.

LOUISE: Listen. It was madness, sheer madness. You must forget, and…

WOODBRIDGE: [*returning*] I beg your pardon, but…

LOUISE: Oh! [*Impatiently*] What is it, Woody?

WOODBRIDGE: Miss Kenny forgot to tell you but after you left yesterday, a wire came from your husband to say he'd be home by the express tonight.

LOUISE: Tonight?

WOODBRIDGE: About due now, isn't it?

LOUISE: [*glancing at her watch*] It's late or he'd be here. I'll have to change. [*Moving away*] Excuse me, won't you? Oh, Don…

DON: I'll be getting along.

LOUISE: No. I want to see you before you go. Give Yarraman a feed and turn him out, will you?

DON: Right.

He goes out by the verandah gate.

LOUISE: Would you ring up the station-master for me, Woody, and find out how the train's running?

WOODBRIDGE: West Range 2, isn't it? [*As she takes off her hat, showing a bandage round her head*] You're hurt, Louise.

LOUISE: [*going indoors*] Nothing to speak of.

WOODBRIDGE: [*at the telephone*] West Range 2, please. Yes. Is that the station-master? Oh, thanks. Could you tell me how the train is running tonight. Late, is she? About ten minutes. But she's signalled now. Thanks. Thanks awfully.

He puts down the receiver. Children troop in, playing Punchinello. MISS KENNY, *coming from the house, puts a cold chookie on the table.*

BILL: Follow me leader. Follow me leader.

MOLLY: [*singing with the children*]
>   Here comes Punchinello, little fellow,
>   What will he do, Punchinello, little dear?

WOODBRIDGE: Can't I play?

MOLLY: We must all do just what Bill does.

> MOLLY *and* WOODBRIDGE *play with the children, jumping, kicking and cutting all manner of crazy capers, while the children sing 'Punchinello'.*

BILL: Now you be Punchinello, Woody, and we'll all follow your leader.

WOODBRIDGE: Right oh.

> *After he has pranced and danced a while, he subsides near* MISS KENNY.

MISS KENNY: It's a wonder she wasn't killed.

WOODBRIDGE: What happened? I don't know yet.

MISS KENNY: I don't know myself. But Don's that worried.

BILL: Let's be wild elephants!

> *The children troop off into the garden with yells and screams of delight.*

LOUISE: [*coming from indoors in a white frock, the bandage gone from her forehead*] That's better. [*Going to the table and kissing* MISS KENNY] Lucretia, you're an angel to have done this for me.

MISS KENNY: I was scared stiff, I don't mind telling you.

LOUISE: And so was I. Yarraman shying like that in the bush. He threw me and bolted. I was unconscious... how long I was unconscious, I don't know. Ugh, and I've got such a headache... [*putting a hand on her heart*] and a pain here.

MISS KENNY: Hadn't we better ring for the doctor?

LOUISE: No. It's all right. See if Don's fixed up Yarraman will you, there's a darling? Tell him I want to see him before he goes.

MISS KENNY: Very well.

> *She trots out.*

LOUISE: [*sitting at the table*] The station-master said the train was signalled, didn't he?

WOODBRIDGE: Louise. What is the meaning of this?

LOUISE: I wish I knew.

WOODBRIDGE: If you don't know, who does?

LOUISE: Listen, Woody. I hadn't the least intention of more than playing with fire, you know. And then, out there... among the trees...

WOODBRIDGE: You were burning off? Getting even with Greg, and the fire got away from you?

LOUISE: Yes. Afterwards, when we were coming home, Yarraman shied and I was thrown. Don had his work cut out to catch him! It was that made us so late.

WOODBRIDGE: Louise!

LOUISE: [*passionately*] I can't feel sorry about it. I won't.

WOODBRIDGE: [*cynically*] An *affaire* of wild-fire passion, eh?

LOUISE: Don't analyse. Don't dissect me.

WOODBRIDGE: That's all right. But what next?

LOUISE: Next?

WOODBRIDGE: You're not in love with this young man. Or are you?

LOUISE: I adore his youth and beauty; that primitive force of his.

WOODBRIDGE: 'Like as the sunflower looks up to the sun.'

LOUISE: Don't Woody.

WOODBRIDGE: I'm surprised at you, my dear. To be caught by a sentimental ballad.

LOUISE: It's not the ballad. It's the thing itself.

WOODBRIDGE: Calf love.

LOUISE: Bushfire love, Woody. The way it blazes, sweeps over the hills, burning away all the old rubbish.

WOODBRIDGE: That's all right so long as it doesn't burn you away too.

LOUISE: What do you mean?

WOODBRIDGE: A *young* man, my dear...

LOUISE: I see...

WOODBRIDGE: Thought you would. The blaze, as you say, may have burnt away a lot of rubbishy repressions. Don't let it get out of hand—blacken and devastate your landscape.

LOUISE: Of course... you're right Woody. Not that I intended to.

WOODBRIDGE: But with blazes—primitive passions—you never know where you are.

LOUISE: Nothing on earth would induce me to leave the children.

WOODBRIDGE: You might not have any choice.

LOUISE: [*indignantly*] Greg would never take the children from me.

WOODBRIDGE: The law's with him.

LOUISE: [*contemptuously*] The law! Of course, I'll have to tell Greg.

WOODBRIDGE: Ask him to forgive you. You'll like doing that?

LOUISE: Woody!

WOODBRIDGE: Well, isn't it what you were after?

LOUISE: It was; but I don't think I'll like it as much as I thought I would.

WOODBRIDGE: How about thinking again? [*As* DON *comes on to the verandah by the gate*] I'll go and help Miss Kenny wash up.

> *He goes off indoors.*

LOUISE: Don!

> *He comes to her and they walk along the verandah to the other end.*

DON: What has he been saying?

LOUISE: Nothing that I did not know.

DON: You can't put me out of your life. I won't go. Not now…

LOUISE: It won't do, Don. You know…

DON: Last night, you said…

LOUISE: Oh, I did. That's why you must go away. [*Bitterly*] I catch fire too easily.

DON: He said that.

LOUISE: It's true, all the same.

DON: For me, it's only, 'all that thou carest to give unto me'.

LOUISE: It wasn't fair, Don, really. I was angry with Greg and grateful to you. You're like a beautiful brown moth that has blown into my life…

DON: And must blow out again. I won't. That's all. You're the white light I've singed my wings in; and will dash against until I die.

LOUISE: Don! [*Hearing a car stop, voices and exclamations*] There's Greg. I must go.

DON: [*catching her arm*] Come again to the creek. [*Savagely*] You will?

LOUISE: It is Greg. They're coming out here.

> DON *jumps over the verandah railing as* GREG *enters from the house at the other end, still coated and with muffler on, the children hanging to him.*

GREG: [*carrying* PEG] But where's Mum?

BILL:

PEG:

BILL: It's my birfday, Dad. What did you bring me for my birfday?

GREG: Oh, there she is. Louise!

LOUISE: Oh, Greg!

She goes to him and kisses him.

GREG: What's up, darling? Anything wrong?

LOUISE: Wrong? No, of course not. Why?

GREG: Didn't want first kiss, eh?

LOUISE: It was fair… to give the children the innings, wasn't it? Bill's birthday.

BILL: It didn't feel like Christmas for my birfday, at all, Dad, till Mummy came home… and Miss Kenny let me devite Jack and Betty and Margot, and Woody…

GREG: Woodbridge? Is he still here?

LOUISE: He goes East in a few days, I think.

BILL: See Dad, what he gave me? A pocket-knife with a corkscrew, and three blades and a toothpick—

GREG: My, that's great, son, isn't it?

BILL: And a file and tweezers, and a spike for getting nails out of horseshoes, and…

GREG: Woodbridge is still *here*, Louise?

LOUISE: He's somewhere about. Been playing wild elephants, with the children.

BILL: Woody's jest tooken Jack and Margot home, Mum.

GREG: Why, Peg's gone to sleep on my shoulder.

LOUISE: Poor mite. I'll put her to bed. [*Cuddling the child as she takes her from* GREG] Little sweeting!

She goes out by the door into the house.

BILL: Come on, Dad. Play blind man's buff with us!

GREG, *taking off his coat and muffler, throws them on a chair. He looks grave and troubled, sensing an atmosphere he does not understand.*

GREG: Right, old man. Who'll be blind man?

BILL: You be blind man, Dad.

> MISS KENNY *comes with tray and coffee from the house.*

GREG: No. [*Tying a handkerchief over the boy's eyes*] You be blind man, Bill… and play a bit with the other chaps, while I have some coffee. [*Going to the table*] Cripes, it's good to be home. [*Drinking his coffee*] Everything all right? How many eggs are we getting? And has Daisy been behaving herself?

MISS KENNY: Best cow ever I see. Brims the pail night and morning. If only she wouldn't swoosh round so with her tail when she's being milked.

GREG: [*laughing*] Does she? And what's the news?

MISS KENNY: News? [*Looking volumes and bursting with indignation*] I could write a book about it.

> *Blind man's buff in full swing, the children rush and shriek past them into the house.*

GREG: Fire away. Has Molly proposed to Mr. Woodbridge yet, or run away with Don? And how are the twins?

> LOUISE *comes on to the verandah again and passes him to fix a lantern. He goes to her.*

Cripes, darling, it's good to be home.

> *He takes her by the shoulder and turns her face to him.* MISS KENNY *retires, Charlestoning discreetly.*

LOUISE: Truly? But you had a good time in Sydney.

GREG: Like hell! I did what I went for. Got old Adamson to stand the money Properjohn needs for development. But I was miserable, all the time.

LOUISE: With so many interesting acquaintances?

GREG: Miserable as a bandicoot. It's no good to me being without you, dearest. I could just blow my damned light out.

LOUISE: But you met your Joybells?

GREG: I did. [*Laughing boyishly*] And she was little, fat—and very sentimental. Expected me to fall on her neck at sight, and—

LOUISE: Didn't you?

GREG: Louise!

LOUISE: Too bad, wasn't it, to raise her expectation like that, and then… not come up to scratch?

GREG: I did better than that. Took Molly's hint and sooled her on to old Adamson. Told her he had pots of money, had fallen in love with her photograph, would give her a good time. God knows what lies. Anyway he did.

LOUISE: What?

GREG: Give her a good time. It felt rather like blackmail when I put my little business proposition to him. But after all, everything's for the best in the best of all possible worlds. Everybody was satisfied. And now it's over and done with you're going to forgive...

LOUISE: Greg, don't say that, for goodness sake.

GREG: [*aghast*] What?

LOUISE: Don't ask me to forgive you. It's I, Greg, I who have to ask...

GREG: All the time I've been away something's been worrying me, Louise, gnawing and gnawing at my brain.

LOUISE: [*with fear*] Greg!

GREG: Giving me no peace, night or day. Is that... [*jerking his head out of doors*] the man you told me of, once?

LOUISE: But?

GREG: [*furiously*] Has he—blast him—has he, laid a finger on you?

LOUISE: Greg!

GREG: Can he fight?

LOUISE: My dear—

GREG: Can he?

LOUISE: Who?

GREG: Woodbridge?

LOUISE: Don't be silly, Greg.

GREG: Then I'll give him a good hiding. These damned literary wasters think they can come messing up a man's home for him. Bad brutes, the whole lot of them!

LOUISE: No. No, it's not Woody at all, Greg. He's been a sort of watchdog while you were away.

GREG: I know the sort of watchdog he's been.

LOUISE: Wouldn't you... wouldn't you... if there was anything to confess... forgive me, Greg?

GREG: [*with consternation*] Forgive you?

LOUISE: If... if...

GREG: Is there?

LOUISE: Greg? Didn't I say you were to be quite free while you were away?

GREG: [*grimly*] You did.

LOUISE: What about our bargain. Wasn't I to be free, too?

GREG: Yes... no. I mean... Louise, you don't mean to tell me that damned blighter—

LOUISE: [*desperately*] No. But—

GREG: Oh well... [*With profound relief*] It's all right!

LOUISE: I might have—

GREG: [*roughly*] Did you... I say... did you go gay with him while I was away?

LOUISE: Greg, you're behaving very badly. What about this humour in the sex relation men are so fond of talking about?

GREG: Humour be damned. You'll see how badly I can behave if—

LOUISE: With somebody else, I was going to say. Supposing—

GREG: It's no good trying to put me off like that. There is nobody else about. No, that won't do my dear.

LOUISE: Greg!

GREG: Tell me you were just trying to pull my leg, make me miserable, to see you could; and I'll say pull away. But I won't be miserable; and... you are going to forget this Joybells business and forgive—

LOUISE: [*wildly*] Don't say that! It's your forgiveness I should be asking for.

WOODBRIDGE *comes in through the verandah gate.*

WOODBRIDGE: Perhaps I'd better...

LOUISE: No, Woody, don't go. He's asked me to forg—

WOODBRIDGE: It's your forgiveness she needs, Reed.

GREG: You dare to stand there and say that to me.

LOUISE: He won't understand. He simply won't understand, Woody!

WOODBRIDGE: I wouldn't try to make him, Louise.

LOUISE: Oh, but—

GREG: If you don't get out of this house at once, sir, I'll kick you out.

WOODBRIDGE: [*tranquilly*] I'm going. But for Louise's sake, and to avoid scandal, let me go unkicked.

LOUISE: It's too bad. I won't have it, Woody—

GREG: God Almighty!

WOODBRIDGE: [*kissing her hand gallantly*] Goodbye, my dear. [*To GREG, whimsically*] I'd give a good deal for you to forgive me… us… Greg. [*Turning just before he goes out*] Supposing you do have to run after your bus again? You've done some great sprints in your day, haven't you?

> *He goes out by the verandah gate. The children romp through yelling and shrieking happily.*

MISS KENNY: [*running in, her hat and coat on*] Mr. Woody! Mr. Woody! Oh, has he gone?

GREG: He has. Come along, you nips, it's time to get a move on.

> *He hustles the children indoors again to get coats and hats.*

MISS KENNY: He promised to have a dance with me.

LOUISE: It was good of you to look after the children for me. [*Kissing her*] And Molly. Where is she?

MISS KENNY: She went. Soon after you came in. I found her crying her heart out in the apple barn. Then she went home.

LOUISE: [*startled*] Molly! Why, what was the matter?

MISS KENNY: [*sarcastically*] She had the toothache—or something—but she wouldn't have had if Don—

GREG: [*coming from the house, two or three children in coats and caps beside him*] These youngsters live near you, don't they, Miss Kenny. Would you mind dropping them on your way home?

MISS KENNY: [*with disappointment*] I may as well, I suppose. [*Going to the door*] Good night, Mrs. Greg.

LOUISE: Good night.

GREG: I'll do as much for you some day, Miss Kenny.

MISS KENNY: [*sparking up*] You never know y'r luck.

GREG: And look here, if you come over some night next week I'll teach you the flat Charleston. Saw them doing it in Sydney.

MISS KENNY: Will you? [*Delightedly*] I'll come. Children, come on.

> *She goes out.*

CHILDREN: Good night. Good night. It's been the beautifulest party.

> *They disappear after* MISS KENNY.

BILL: Good night.

LOUISE: Good night. [*as* BILL *comes to kiss her*] You must trot off to bed now, Bill darling.

> *He goes by way of the supper table, helps himself to sweets and a banana, after which he falls asleep in a chair.*

GREG: [*standing over her, more in sorrow than in anger*] Louise! Louise!

LOUISE: [*helplessly*] Greg!

> DON *is heard singing on the road.*

GREG: Tell me you don't want to go after him.

LOUISE: [*startled*] Who?

GREG: Woodbridge, of course.

LOUISE: No. [*Thinking away from him*] I don't want to…

GREG: I couldn't let you. I won't. [*Putting his arms round her, very tenderly*] We'll forget… this… and begin all over again.

> *She strains away as a phrase of* DON*'s singing comes between them.*

What is it?

DON: [*singing in the distance*]

> 'All that I ask for is all that may be,
> All that thou carest to give unto me…'

GREG: [*savagely*] Cripes, does he think he's the only man in the world can sing that blasted song? [*Taking up the air and bellowing extravagantly*]

> 'Then as the sunflow'r looks up to the light,
> Sad in its absence and glad in its sight,
> I can look up to thee, morning and night,
> And love thee forever,
> Love thee for ever and ever…'

LOUISE: [*laughing and semi-vanquished, as he takes her in a bear's hug*] Greg!

END OF PLAY

BRUMBY INNES

*Dennis Miller (Brumby) attacks Vic Marsh (John Hallinan) while Lynette
Curran (May) looks on, in the Channel 0/10 Network production, Melbourne
1973, with the Australian Performing Group and the Nindethana Theatre.
Photo by courtesy Channel 0.*

Author's preface to the 1940 edition

The staging of the corroboree should not present too great difficulties. Gramophone records of the airs sung are available, and the mimodrame, gestures and dancing, although of a strange wild grace, are simple enough. The corroboree in this play is used to give something of the dignity, beauty and mystery of a primitive people in their natural surroundings: against their appearance under the conditions of a vanquished race.

Polly is a Hecuba in bronze: the tragedy of the vanquished Trojans, the tragedy of the Aboriginals in the Nor'–west. Americans are depicting the Negroes in music and in the theatre, and it should not be impossible for players to give the natives of Australia, seriously, and with sympathy. All the men and women of the tribe in this play are studies from life. If, however, the corroboree makes for insuperable difficulties, Act I may be reduced to a suggestion of the blacks' camp and the women sitting and clicking sticks, about the fire.

Words sung to the corroboree are treasure really. The Aboriginals seem reluctant to tell them, superstitious of unravelling their mystery, perhaps. Often the words they sing are not words of their everyday language. Many of the corroboree songs, or tabee, are in a dead language, I think… hereditary legends and saga drifted down from remote ages; others are inspirational, sung by the yinerrie, inventor of corroborees, or poet of the tribe, and director of ceremonies, as the spirit moves him.

Only folk reared on isolated stations who have had lifelong associations with the blacks, or a native who has broken with his people and traditions, are able to gather some of these songs and to tell us their meaning. 'The Song of the Stranger' and 'The Song of the Mate' in Act One are both authentic fragments in an ancient language of the Gnulloonga tribe. Words of the narloo corroboree are in a local dialect. The gins seemed afraid to give me the ancient words. They would only say: 'Sing go away narloo… come dark', waving to the hills. 'Narloo, eagle–hawk… like smoke… moon, maybe.'

One writes as one must: produces as one may. Which is to say, the language of a Nor'–westerner must be tempered to the ears of city dwellers—so be it! The same applies to the song in Act II. Sung by a stockman under the stars you would not miss a word; but as little or as much may be used as the play will carry.

Katharine Susannah Prichard

Peter Cummins (Jack Carey) and Dennis Miller in the Channel 0/10 production. Photo by courtesy Channel 0.

Brumby Innes

Introduction to the 2018 edition

It is disturbing to read *Brumby Innes* in the context of the 'Me Too' movement that seeks to bring silenced stories forward about sexual abuse and exploitation of women in situations where they are denied power. Despite all the changes over the past century some things have not gone beyond superficial changes. Katharine Susannah Prichard (1883-1969) wrote *Brumby Innes* in 1927—91 years ago—foregrounding the sexual abuse and exploitation of women in contexts where their vulnerability and accepted social practices gave them no protection.

As a writer, Prichard had a strong commitment to and concern for ordinary working people, particularly women. This informed all her work. Primarily a novelist and political writer, her plays were often a working of material she later used in her novels. Despite her focus on other writings, Prichard wrote 17 plays altogether. Many of them were one-act works. Her short plays are often agitprop pieces and realist drama dealing starkly with women's rights, industrial conditions and women's suffering in war. An early example of her political questioning was her first play, *The Burglar* (1910). A one-act comedy, *The Burglar* is an entertaining encounter between a girl with socialist pretensions, and an upwardly mobile young man who is financing his university studies by stealing. Her next plays, *Her Place* (1913) and *For Instance* (1914), were first produced in London, by the Actresses' Franchise League. *The Great Man*, a three-act comedy about a baby, was produced by the Pioneer Players in Melbourne in 1923.

Another recurring theme in her work is race relations in Australia. Focused on the themes of women's rights and racism, Prichard's three-act drama *Brumby Innes* (1927) is her most significant play. Drawing on personal experience of time spent in the Kimberly in Western Australia, the play deals with images and expectations of masculinity and femininity and Australian race relations, particularly between European settlers and Indigenous Australians. Brumby, bearing the common name for a wild horse, is an arrogant self-proclaimed bushman, who sees women as there to serve him and his needs. Prichard based the character of Brumby on a man she met when she was in Western Australia. He struck her so forcibly as the epitome of a particular type of man and values that she developed her concept of him further in her novel *Coonardoo*, which was published in a serialised form in the *Bulletin* in 1928, a year after finishing *Brumby Innes*. The characterisation of Brumby in the 1920s was a direct challenge to the image of the Australian man of the bush celebrated since the 1890s, who was seen as a resourceful, honorable, independent man who trusted only his mates. This figure dominated the Australian imagination, producing a white racialised, masculine norm of the real Australian. This was then co-opted to define the figure of the ANZAC digger in World War I.

The play depicts three women, two Indigenous, Polly and Wylba, and one non-Indigenous, May—all totally at the mercy of Brumby. They are, according to him, 'his mares'. This belief and level of control is condoned by the other men because, 'Brum ain't unkind to his women'. The powerlessness of the Indigenous Australians before Brumby's abuse is paralleled in the powerlessness of the white woman before his assumption of his exclusive right to choose and his casual brutality.

Prichard's play is almost unique for white writers at the time, in setting the initial scenes of the play within the Aboriginal world. The play opens with a corroboree that is distinct from decades of previous white renditions on stage. Aboriginal corroborees were usually limited to shouting and stomping around a fire in the shadows or off stage. One of the innovative features of the play is the use of an Aboriginal language from the Kimberly, the Ngaala-warngga of South Pandjima, in the lines of the Indigenous characters, rather than either silence or some form of imaginary pidgin as was the usual practice in previous drama texts by white writers. Prichard spent time in the Kimberly where she learnt the Aboriginal words for both conversation and of public corroboree songs.[1] Linguists have critiqued Prichard's documenting of the language in part because she was there for a relatively brief time without any previous experience of documenting languages or in-depth knowledge of Aboriginal cultures in general. Regardless of shortcomings and changes in spelling Aboriginal words,

Prichard documented and incorporated into *Brumby Innes* three public corroboree songs and dances with a high level of accuracy.

The opening scene claims the performance space both visually and aurally for the Indigenous presence. For Prichard, 'the corroboree is used to give something of the dignity, beauty and mystery of a primitive people under the condition of a vanquished race.' Though her language resonates with contemporaneous views of Aboriginal people, there is a respect and recognition of shared humanity and potential that is usually lacking in other works of this period.

The early scenes where Brumby beats Polly and takes Wylba, a young Aboriginal girl, from her people's camp, shooting any Aboriginal man who opposes him, are confronting. Paralleling the treatment of the two Aboriginal women is the figure of May. She is a young white woman visiting a relative, meeting new men and experimenting with flirting and her own developing sexual power. Brumby believes her growing sense of self gives him the right to rape her and force her into marriage because he wants a white wife as well as his Aboriginal victims.

In 1927, Katharine Susannah Prichard won a contest in *Triad* magazine with *Brumby Innes* and a production was promised but never eventuated. The content was considered too shocking. The play was not produced until 1972. The production was a collaboration between the Australian Performing Group and Nindethana, an Aboriginal theatre company in Melbourne.

The cast of *Brumby Innes* included Harry Williams, Joyce Johnson, Jack Charles, Bert Williams, Ian Johnson, Bernie Hoffman, Monica Hoffman, Elizabeth Hoffman, Val Power, Marcia Briggs, Dennis Miller, Peter Cummins, Vic Marsh and Lynette Curran.[2] The season of *Brumby Innes* in November 1972 was so successful a grant was sought and received to film the production.[3] It was filmed at Channel O (known later as Channel 10) and went to air in June 1973.[4]

Prichard was ahead of her times with Brumby Innes in myriad ways. In the first decades of the 20th century other writers, especially those central to the Pioneer Players such as Louis Esson, were seeking to celebrate a racialised, masculine nationalism that was particularly expressed through bush myths and comedies. In the 1920s and 1930s women writers such as Betty Roland and Henrietta Drake-Brockman were changing the frame of reference to engage with the complexities of social existence. It was not until the 1930s that others sought to critique Australian society and race relations, revealing a broader range of masculinities and in effect interrogating the mythology of the bush from different political perspectives and with different intentions. None sought to stage unpalatable truths with the same uncompromising clarity as Prichard did in *Brumby Innes*.

Maryrose Casey

Maryrose Casey is an Associate Professor with the Monash Indigenous Studies Centre. She has published widely on Indigenous Australian theatre and performance. Her major publications include the multi-award winning books *Creating Frames: Contemporary Indigenous Theatre* (2004) and *Telling Stories: Aboriginal and Torres Strait Islander Performance* (2012).

[1] Aboriginal performances including song and dance and be divided into different categories, secret and sacred, public Dreaming stories that are often simpler versions of secret stories and aim at educating and thirdly topical performances for entertainment.

[2] Brumby Innes Program Australian Performing Group and Nindethana Theatre 1972.

[3] Australian Performing Group Internal Bulletin No 3 1972

[4] Advertisement, Newspaper Reports and letters APG Archives Box 47, State Library Victoria.

Brumby Innes

Shifting the focus of the white gaze

With *Brumby Innes*, Katharine Susannah Prichard elicits an image of the north-west landscape that is both vibrant and authentic. Her poetic metaphors are stunning. The plots and subplots are like trails of breadcrumbs leading the reader into a social, historical and psychological exploration of white Australia's association with Indigenous Australia. As a teacher-linguist who has worked on Indigenous language, cultural and interpreting programs with Nyangumarta people living in the Pilbara, I reveled in Prichard's unequivocal use of Indigenous words. Indeed, she launches the play with language, Aboriginal speech, misspelt by modern orthography standards, but authentic all the same. She's an author who has clearly done her research. But, despite this, *Brumby Innes* wasn't an easy play for me to read.

Brumby Innes takes place in 1929 at Karraka, a remote cattle station in the Pilbara, located in the north of Western Australia. It is the homestead of the main character: Brumby Innes. Essentially, the play is a critical commentary on gender and racial inequality. In Brumby's company are: the old white stockman Jack; the thirteen-year-old Aboriginal girl Wylba; Brumby's Aboriginal mistress Polly (who works at the homestead); the white cattle station owner John; and John's niece (who is subsequently Brumby's wife) May. Brumby is a hard-drinking, violent yet vibrant man who is determined to fulfill his wants with force and no thought for the repercussions his actions may have on others.

It wasn't just the storyline that made me feel uneasy. It cut a lot deeper than that. For starters, Prichard appropriates a law ceremony to begin her play. It was first performed by the Australian Performing Group and Nindethana Theatre at the Pram Factory, Melbourne in November 1972. Although the Pram Factory was a trail-blazer in that it invited an Aboriginal theatre group to the stage, the thought of a law ceremony uprooted from the red earth of the Pilbara and performed in the land of the Kulin nation, with no cultural direction or vetting from traditional owners, does not rest well with me. In the broader context of white Australia's appropriation (some might call it theft) of Indigenous property—skulls and ancestral remains, secret-sacred objects, implements, artwork and children, to name a few—it takes on a whole new meaning, on which I will elaborate further in this introduction.

Then there's this passage of dialogue describing how Brumby Innes is let off a charge for having sexual relations with an underage Aboriginal girl:

JOHN: He'd've gone up for nine or ten years, for a dead cert'…

JACK: On the age of the girl?

JOHN: Told the magistrate himself, she was thirteen and three months.

JACK: You didn't do that, Brum?

JOHN: Got round the town before he went to court. Did my best to get him there sober, Jack, but it was no use.

BRUMBY: [*crowing and imitating the magistrate*] 'How can you say the girl's age is sixteen, Mr. Hallinan, when as a matter of fact, the defendant states the age of the girl to be thirteen years and three months? If he didn't know—wasn't sure—why should he say three months?'

JACK: Did you say she was sixteen, John?

JOHN: I did. That's what I reck'n her age is…

BRUMBY: [*continuing his recitation*] 'Oh,' says he, lyin' like a tripe hound. 'I know she's sixteen because I saw her. She was livin' with her people on the Creek first time I come through with cattle ten years ago. She was six or seven then—couldn't be less. I been on Nyedee ten years next January, and…'

JACK: That got him off, John.   *(pp103-104)*

There is no doubt that Pritchard inserted this scene to show just how above the law white men were during the 1920s, especially when they were far removed from mainstream white society. But the effect of the repeated rape on the thirteen-year-old Wylba is not known. Polly and even Jack's reactions indicate they believe she had it coming to her. In their eyes, Brumby's stealing of cattle is far more reprehensible than the rape and kidnap of an Aboriginal minor.

Prichard's insinuation that Aboriginal people are a dying race, unable to adapt and reliant on white Australia to survive, is highly contentious. And I know it's a sign of the context in which she writes, but Prichard doesn't hold back on using racist words like 'native', 'gin', 'blacks', 'niggers' and 'abos'. This, coupled with Aboriginal characters being portrayed as a cross between mistreated pets and simple-yet-defiant children, makes me cringe. Polly is the only Aboriginal character who defies this portrayal, yet despite her overtly contemptuous stance and her speaking out against Brumby's actions, she is unable or unwilling to escape Brumby's incarceration of her on the homestead and fiercely defends his actions over those of her own people.

Here's an example of how many of the Aboriginal characters in *Brumby Innes* are portrayed:

> *She gives the tobacco, at which the old woman beams, and turns to go, without thanks, as is the native fashion. She stumbles at the door, groping her way with hands before her.* POLLY *follows her out. They are heard jabbering outside, their voices shrill and quarrelsome. Another native woman turns around the doorpost on the right, with an eye cocked to be sure* POLLY *has not seen her. She is of average height, fat and jolly looking, in a tawny, dust–coloured skirt, man's hat and coat.*

Oh, it's you, Warrarie! What do you want?

WARRARIE: [*ingratiatingly*] Got'm t'read, missus?

MAY: What for… you want thread, Warrarie?

WARRARIE: [*turning and showing brown limbs through a very torn skirt*] Weary booger, dress.

MAY: [*laughing*] I should think so.

WARRARIE: Poor booger me. [*Wheedlingly*] Got'm gina–gina store miah, meetchie?

MAY: A new dress? What on earth do you want a new gina–gina for?

WARRARIE: [*gurgling, coy and sly, hugging herself*] Got'm noova.

MAY: Noova… a lover?   *(pp99-100)*

My discomfort here stems from the implications of a non-Indigenous writer using narrative positioning to characterise Indigenous people and culture in whatever way she chooses. This is shown in May's reaction to Warrarie wanting a new dress. I learned much from the Nyangumarta people during my teaching stint in the desert; of particular note was their extraordinary resourcefulness. That's why they have been able to thrive for tens of thousands of years. Nowhere in *Brumby Innes* is captured Aboriginal peoples' ability to use whatever is at hand and adapt to change, and hang onto or restore traditional belief and value systems. The words 'jabbering', 'wheedlingly' and 'gurgling' explicitly misrepresent these important skills.

Until very recently, this was the view to which the majority of the reading public had access. It is the dominant voice of non-Indigenous people representing Indigenous people. Historically, it was rare to have Aboriginal people speaking for and about themselves. Their voices were overrun by ill-informed and self-proclaimed experts. Because the opinions of these people were the loudest and most prevalent, they were often mistaken for the truth. *Brumby Innes* may be clichéd and misrepresentative by today's standards, but if we look at the play in the broader context of when it was written, it is much bigger than the sum of its parts.

Australia was a very different country in 1940, when *Brumby Innes* was first published. It had just entered World War II and had only just clawed its way out of the Great Depression. When Prichard was a young journalist, she listened to reports of the Anti-Sweating League, and heard the evidence of girls who worked long hours on high-pressure machines for minimum wages. With their husbands out of work or ill, and having no money to buy food and clothes for a young family, these women were forced to submit to the whims of unscrupulous employers to get work, earning just over a shilling for making a dozen nightgowns. In her 1956 article 'Why I am a Communist', Prichard asks, 'How was it that some people should have to live in fear and poverty … while others … could live easily and pleasantly, squandering riches, and concerned only about their own pleasure and power?' This question of social injustice and gender inequality is what she attempts to address in *Brumby Innes*.

What was the reality for Aboriginal people at the time *Brumby Innes* was published? They were banned from entering central business districts in cities and some regional towns without holding special permits. They were killed *en masse*, in massacres like the one that occurred at Coniston cattle station in the Northern Territory, in actions that courts ruled were justified. In the 1930s and 40s Aboriginal people required permission to get married. They weren't allowed to speak their own language or practise their own culture. They were not paid appropriately for their work on pastoral properties or in government missions. They couldn't buy houses or land. They were denied access to higher education and given menial jobs, which paid little or nothing at all. Women and girls suffered repeated sexual abuse. When *Brumby Innes* was published, Aboriginal people had endured 35 years of an assimilation policy that saw children fathered by non-Aboriginal men taken away from their Aboriginal families to be bought up in brutal institutions, and trained as cheap domestic workers. These people are now known as the Stolen Generations.

The reality of Indigenous peoples' lives was not reflected in works of Australian fiction at the time. Emphasis was placed on settlers battling courageously against a backdrop of natural hazards, Aboriginal people being among them. There was also fiction that mocked Indigenous Australians, and a spate of romantic narratives trivialising their history as a bygone era, in nostalgic recollections. Sometimes, Aboriginal characters were used in a tokenistic sense, depicted as a homogenous group of 'blacks' or 'natives'. The 'black velvet' sexual metaphor of Aboriginal women—designed to assert their exoticism to white men—was also part of this literature. On the whole, there was very little attempt to question accepted stereotypes. Rarely were Aboriginal people portrayed as distinct characters. *Brumby Innes* railed against all that. By having Aboriginal characters as identifiable entities with human traits, Prichard flips the coin from exoticism to exploitation.

Brumby Innes was a precursor to Prichard's famous novel, *Coonardoo*. The play was written before *Coonardoo*, but the novel was published first in 1929 (in serial form in *The Bulletin*, under the name of Jim Ashburton). You can imagine the impact the novel must have had, given the state of literature at the time. People were shocked to the core; *The Bulletin* received hundreds of letters of protest. More progressive writers, such as Vance Palmer, were worried that Prichard would ruin their chances of having more candid works published in the future. Instead, the opposite happened—she paved the way for a type of fiction that tried to capture the interior life of Aboriginal characters and/

or represented them as social beings. Prichard, for better or worse, was instrumental in driving a largely ignored or grossly misrepresented issue to a place of social protest in Australian literature. Although far from perfect in today's political climate, both *Coonardoo* and *Brumby Innes* attempted to challenge the conventional modes of Australian writing. Although *Brumby Innes* was published in 1940, it wasn't performed until 1972. Even then, as Australian playwright John Romeril writes in *Australian Theatre History: The Australian Performing Group at the Pram Factory,* the play struck a blow and 'showed Australia that great plays had been penned in this country but scandalously ignored'. In staging the play, the Pram Factory also 'beckoned Nindethana onto the stage, Victoria's first "modern" Aboriginal theatre group who for some years continued to use our premises'.

In 2008, I wrote a PhD exegesis about the ethics of non-Indigenous people representing Australia's Indigenous people in works of fiction. The writing explored the intersections between ethics, politics and storytelling. I suggested that fiction writers from Australia's dominant culture had a responsibility that underpinned their representation of Aboriginal people. Being accountable was key, not only for what was written but also the effect generated by our words. I asked writers to have a crack at seeing beyond the prevailing discourse of 'the other'. Listening to those who have been silenced, taken away, abused and divided was part of that challenge.

As well as being able to write a good story, Prichard's journalistic background provided the impetus to conduct extensive research. She took herself off to Turee station in the Pilbara (Banyjima / Pandjima country) and lived there for a time, moving beyond the confines of the homestead and into the 'uloo' where Aboriginal people lived. While *Brumby Innes* is Prichard's 'version' of the facts, we are reading something based on research, as opposed to the imagined fantasy of many other authors of the time. Judging from her writing, it is clear she watched, asked questions, and listened to Aboriginal people, just like she did with the girls from the Anti-Sweating League.

To witness the bravery with which Prichard portrayed non-Indigenous Australians in an unsavoury light, readers need go no further than the character of Brumby Innes himself. Brumby is a lecherous drunk who owns Karraka cattle station and everyone within its boundary. This is shown particularly in the first act, where, defying the warning of his head stockman, he brazenly invades an important Aboriginal ceremony to snatch Wylba for his own sexual benefit and tries to shoot anyone, including the Aboriginal man the girl has been promised to in marriage, who stands in the way. He is much hated and feared by Aboriginal men, Wylba, May, and to some extent, Polly. Prichard really went out on a limb with Innes. It is little wonder that her play was not performed until more than 30 years after it was published.

There is one word that was central to my argument in my exegesis: entanglement. It comes from Nicholas Thomas, an anthropologist with a passionate interest in art. In *Entangled Objects: Exchange, Material Culture and Colonialism in the Pacific* (Harvard University Press, 1991), Thomas uses the concept of 'mutual entanglement' to show how modern anthropological paradigms fail to capture the complex relations that occur when different cultures come into contact with each other. Entanglement acknowledges diversity both within and between Indigenous and non-Indigenous cultures. It resists the notion of Indigenous people always inhabiting completely separate domains to non-Indigenous people, without collapsing the two groups into each other. It's a concept that helps us to break away from stereotypes and binaries—the black and white, them and us sort of thing. Stereotypes mean we can take sides and cheer on our own team. We don't need to question the logic or indeed the 'reality' of these perceived constructions. In *Brumby Innes*, Prichard takes a step towards acknowledging how enormously complex, multi-layered and different black and white Australia is, and how entwined the relationships between us are.

Let's re-visit the character of Brumby. He treats his women and the Aboriginal people who work for him worse than the cattle and horses on his station. Attempted murder, assault and rape are just some of the charges he'd be up against today. He would also be acknowledged as a paedophile. Yet nowhere is he brought to justice. He blatantly ignores advice and warnings from the white men in the play, who at least provide some moral compass for his actions. Brumby swings between being a loveable-yet-drunken blaggard and a bully. But when it comes to the crunch—like when he is called to court for having sexual relations with an underage girl—the white men stick together. Even John, the most moral of them, lies to get Brumby off the hook and organises for him to marry his niece. Brumby operates outside the law on all levels: white and black, morally, ethically and legally; and no-one in the play is able to bring him to justice or make him recognise his prejudice. Sure, characters can scratch a sore (like stealing from stores, refusing to kiss him, or bailing him up for stealing their livestock), but essentially he's untouchable and with that he earns a grudging respect from the other characters.

The depiction of the female characters is also complicated. Brumby entrusts his mistress Polly with the running of the homestead. Her elevated status compared to the rest of the Aboriginal characters, including the men, infuriates Brumby's wife May. (Although May, as a white woman, occupies a higher position than Polly, they are mistreated in the same way by Brumby, yet because of jealous rivalry they are unable to support each other in their captivity.) Polly's treatment of her own people is a source of mystery to me. It points to an elevated status which she values above and beyond any kinship ties. She sees the continual rape of Wylba by Brumby as a natural result of the girl's flirtatious nature. It's possible that Polly is from another region and therefore has no affiliation with the Banyjima / Pandjima people of Karraka. On the other hand, May's treatment of Aboriginal characters other than Polly, while patronising in today's terms, is friendly. It's impossible to determine if this is her way of infuriating Polly and undermining her position, or a way of quenching her own loneliness. Maybe it's a little bit of both, but the fact remains that there are no binaries here; the situation at the Brumby Innes homestead is impossibly entangled.

As readers, it is important to situate texts within historical contexts. It helps us to deal with the ideas and beliefs that shape our thoughts about culture. We are blessed today to have access to a multitude of stories written and voiced by Aboriginal people, such as *Raparapa: Stories from the Fitzroy River Drovers* (Marshall 2011), *A Town is Born: The Fitzroy Crossing Story* (Hawke 2013), and *I Am An Artist. I Come From The Bush*, an ABC Open project of thirteen short biographic films. These are stories about station life told by Aboriginal stockmen, women and domestics who lived and grew up on north-west cattle stations. *Brumby Innes,* taken in conjunction with these kinds of stories, can provide a context that reveals a complex and entangled history.

To me, *Brumby Innes* is more than a play that captures the deep-seated prejudice of white Australia through a story about interracial sexuality. Despite its challenges, it is a milestone that marks a shift in thinking, and a reminder of how literature can challenge and change perceptions, and shift the focus of our gaze to something that can lead to change.

Jacqueline Wright

Jacqueline Wright has a creative arts doctorate from Curtin University where she is an Adjunct Fellow. Her first novel, *Red Dirt Talking*, won the 2010 TAG Hungerford Award and was longlisted for the 2013 Miles Franklin. Parts of *Red Dirt Talking* have also been adapted for radio and stage. She has since published short stories and creative non-fiction pieces in *Knitting and Other Stories* (MRP), *Kimberley Stories*, *Summer Lovin'*, *Purple Prose* (FP), *Looking West* (Griffith Review) and *Westerly 61.1* (UWA Press). Jacqueline is currently working on her second novel.

Referenced Works

Australian Broadcasting Commission 2011 and 2014. *I Am An Artist. I Come From The Bush*, TV show, series 1 and 2, ABC Open.

Hawke, S. 2013. *A Town is Born: The Fitzroy Crossing Story*, Magabala Books, Broome.

Marshall, P. (ed.) 2011. *Raparapa: Stories from the Fitzroy River Drovers*, Magabala Books, Broome.

Prichard, K. S. 1956. *Why I am a Communist*, Current Book Distributors (Communist Party of Australia), Sydney.

Romeril, J. (viewed April 18, 2018). *Last words on a nearly made it theatre: Memoir of a survivor,* The Pram Factory, www.pramfactory.com/memoirsfolder/Romeril-John.html

Thomas, N. 1991. *Entangled Objects: Exchange, Material Culture, and Colonialism in the Pacific*, Harvard University Press, Cambridge.

.

Brumby Innes was first performed by the Australian Performing Group and Nindethana Theatre at the Pram Factory, Melbourne, on 1 November 1972, with the following cast:

WONGANA	Harry Williams
MICKINA	Ian Johnson
SPIDER	Bert Williams
GINARRA	Ian Johnson
OLD JIMMY	Jack Charles
MUNGA	Bernie Hoffmann
TULLAMURRA	Elizabeth Hoffmann
NARDADU	Joyce Johnson
WARRARIE	Val Power
WYLBA	Monica Hoffmann
POLLY	Marcia Briggs
BRUMBY INNES	Dennis Miller
JACK CAREY	Peter Cummins
JOHN HALLINAN	Vic Marsh
MAY HALLINAN	Lynette Curran

Setting designed by Helen Pitt
Directed by John Smythe

CHARACTERS

WONGANA
MICKINA
SPIDER   } Aboriginal men
OLD JIMMY
MUNGA

TULLAMURRA
NARDADU
WARRARIE   } Aboriginal women
WYLBA
POLLY

BRUMBY INNES
JACK CAREY   An old stockman
JOHN HALLINAN   Owner of Nyedee Station
MAY HALLINAN   His niece

ACT ONE
The blacks' camp.

ACT TWO
The kitchen of Brumby Innes' homestead on a wild and
lonely cattle station of north–west Australia.

ACT THREE
The same, three months later.

PUBLISHERS' NOTE (2018)
The play, including stage directions, has been reproduced exactly
as it was written in 1927. We recognise that much of the language,
including Prichard's own words, is not acceptable for common usage
today. The play appears as is, in the hope of exposing the difficulties
of colonial history, including the racism inherent in the language of
those who would have seen themselves as allies. This play shows how
discourse has changed across the years.

ACT ONE

Under a wide stretch of starlit sky, native women and children are sitting in two rows at a little distance from the camp fire, burning low. Opposite, on the left, a sun-dried bullock's hide is stretched between a tall, spindling mulga and two or three low–growing bushes, to form a screen for the men who are painting themselves with white clay, making long curly lines on their legs, and circles, or squares with spots inside, on their breasts. A huge face, cut from the chalk–white bark of a river gum, is lying on the ground. The men are naked but for wandy cloths, three–quarter wise in front, a string between the buttocks. An old man, very fat, has a tuft of emu feathers tied on like a tail behind. MICKINA, *a handsome stalwart young black, wears parrot feathers under an armlet on his left arm and swathed around his head, showing red and green. Two or three kangaroo dogs prowl about the fire and among the women and children. The plain is bare to the far horizon where a line of low–growing scrub touches the starlit sky.*

WONGANA, *in his everyday clothes and hat of a station stockman, comes from behind a screen where the men are getting ready for the corroboree, and crosses to the women and children. He is the man of authority and director of ceremonies, good–looking and powerful; older, more mature than* MICKINA. *He sits cross–legged at the end of the front row of women, picks up kylies, and clicking them rhythmically, begins to sing in a full, melodious alto. The women sing with him in a slightly higher key, beating small sticks together.*

WONGANA: Balgarilla mardoo mardourie yiendie warilla…
WOMEN: Balgarilla mardoo mardourie yiendie warilla…

> *Then* WONGANA, *the* WOMEN *and* CHILDREN *sing the line together, repeating it many times, but varying the key each time. When the singing dies away there is silence for a moment.* NARDADU, *a grandmother of the tribe, in an old skirt, man's coat and hat, stands up at the further end of the front row of women, a long stick in her hand, and waves it towards the bullock hide where the men going to corroboree are.*

WONGANA: [*clicking and singing again*] Balgarilla mardoo…

> WOMEN *and* CHILDREN *join in; but the singing takes on a tone of incitement, jeering, as if to say:* 'Come along, you fellows!' 'What's the matter?' 'Are you frightened?' 'Don't be shy!' 'Let's have a look at you!'

> SPIDER *appears from behind the bullock hide, followed by the rest of the men. Tall, agile, the most adept and experienced dancer,* SPIDER *stands in the attitude of a man in a strange country, looking about him, throwing out both arms in the native gesture of surprise; begins to dance with little jiggling steps as if walking or running quickly, then like a kangaroo scenting water, hops forward, legs bowed, arms loose, prancing first on one leg, then on the other, coming down on both together with the thud of a kangaroo's tail. All with rhythm and stark wild grace to the women's singing. At the fire, though, as if the step were finished, no audience there, he turns and walks back to the bullock hide. Each of the men imitates closely every movement of the leader.* MICKINA, *muscular and dandyish;* MUNGA, *boyish, undeveloped, watching anxiously what the others are doing;* GINARRA, *sturdy, well-formed;* OLD JIMMY, *pot-bellied, with slender legs, the emu's feathers bobbing behind him. Each of the men does the step singly; then in a row, and around the fire, walking back behind the bullock hide when it is finished, in everyday fashion.*

> *One of the dogs, springing out, goes for* OLD JIMMY's *emu feathers, and is driven off angrily by* NARDADU, *causing a drift of laughter among the women and children. But the occasion is one of high seriousness, dancers absorbed in their interpretation of these songs in a dead language which have come to them from bygone generations of their people. Singers are under the influence of the night and the secret, mysterious movins, or charms, in the songs they are singing.*

WONGANA: [*clicking the kylies, giving the rhythm of the next dance, to a slightly different melody*] Narloo, narloo… gindoo bun abbie…

> *The women and children join in, repeating the line as before. From the darkness beyond the firelight,* SPIDER *as the narloo*

comes hopping. He seems to come from the horizon, a crouched figure, hopping low, like a frog, all his bones outlined with white, a huge face of white bark over his head. A fearsome figure, he hops and crouches right up to the fire, peers at the women and children. Still singing, their voices quivering with fear and excitement, they watch him, beating their sticks. NARDADU's *voice shrills out as she steps forward and threatens the narloo with her stick. Singing of the women vibrates to the charm they are trying to use against the narloo. The narloo wavers before the old woman's threatening figure and upheld stick. He retreats backwards, thwarted, intimidated, and hops off into darkness across the plains again while the singing of the women takes on a tone of derision and triumph. The singing dies away, voices wandering into silence, dropping out one by one, until* NARDADU's *are the last low notes.* NARDADU *puts more wood on the fire.*

WONGANA: [*Clicking and singing*] Narloo, narloo… gindoo bun abbie.
WOMEN: Narloo, narloo… gindoo bun abbie.
  Warieda munga murnda bun abbie.

The first line is repeated as before. A flock of narloos, the rest of the men from behind the bullock hide, their faces whitened and white feathers in their hair, run up to the fire. They dance, hovering and fluttering like white cockatoos. The women drive them off and the singing dies away.

Before the next dance, the women turn their backs to the camp fire, crouching against the earth. WONGANA *spreads old grey dirty blankets over them. No native woman must see this corroboree. When* WONGANA *clicks and sings, the women join him in muffled tones.*

WONGANA: [*clicking and singing*] Ubi! Ubi!…
WOMEN: Ubi! Ubi!… hebina hawiah!
  Wara lunghia bina hawiah!

SPIDER, *a high white head–dress like a spider's web, erect from his head and jutting over his forehead, comes from the bullock hide. He gestures and dances before the fire with gaiety and an abandon which suggests the Dionysia, working himself into such a frenzy that he stands shivering, overwrought. Men behind the bullock hide join in the singing, rush to join* SPIDER *and dance beside him, shivering, shaking themselves, stamping, shouting and singing.*

ALL: Ubi! Ubi!… hebina hawiah!
    Wara lunghia bina hawiah!

While the excitement is at its height, BRUMBY INNES *staggers in from the left. He is drunk; a powerful man, handsome and attractive in a rough and brutal way, wearing well–worn buff trousers, loose cotton shirt, with leather belt, matchbox attached, pipe stuck through, revolver in a leather case, widebrimmed felt hat and elastic–sided boots, the ends pulled over his trousers.*

BRUMBY: [*swaggering into the firelight*] Wylba! Hi, there, Wylba!

SPIDER *retreats from the fire; the rest of the men surge forward. Women throw back their blankets.*

WONGANA: [*facing* BRUMBY *angrily*] Wiah! No, Brumby!
BRUMBY: Wylba? Where is she? Want… Wylba.

A girl among the native women, very slight and childish–looking, draws attention to herself by shrieking and shrinking against NARDADU.

MICKINA: [*striding over to stand beside* WONGANA, *the other men following him, defensive and aggressive*] Wylba stay camp.
BRUMBY: [*seeing the girl, without paying the least attention to the men*] There you are! [*Staggering over to her*] Wylba… you come with me, Wylba.
WYLBA: [*shrinking and clinging to the old woman*] Wiah! Wiah!
WONGANA: [*going to* BRUMBY, *humouring him, but with dignity*] You go back, Brumby. Boys, angry. Say Wylba stay camp… not go with you.
BRUMBY: [*roaring*] What?
WONGANA: [*repeating*] You go back. Boys badgee. Say Wylba stay here… not go… with you…
BRUMBY: Not go with me?
WONGANA: Boys angry. Bita muna you, Brumby.

BRUMBY: Fed up with me, are they? Christ, what's this place comin' to, I'd like to know. Who's boss here? I'll show 'em.

He goes over and tugs the girl from the women. MICKINA *bounds over and wrenches her from him.*

WONGANA: [*coming between them*] Better go, Brum. Boys won't give up this girl.

BRUMBY: [*pulling the revolver from his belt*] Won't give her up, won't they? We'll see if they won't give her up...

A spear whistles and plunges into the ground beside him.

That's it, is it? Young bucks down this uloo think they... got everything their own way... Keep the women to themselves. Where do I come in? That's what I want to know. [*Covering* MICKINA *with his revolver*] Leave her go, or I'll shoot. [*As the native releases the girl*] What's she got to do with you, anyhow? [*To* WONGANA] Is she his woman?

JACK CAREY *enters from left front, running and stumbling blindly. He is an old stockman and teamster, very tall, over eighty and nearly blind. He wears faded blue dungarees, a loose greyish white shirt, elastic–sided boots and belt of a stockman, but has come hatless in his hurry.*

WONGANA: No. Promised one.

JACK: Brumby!

BRUMBY: Well! [*Laughing hilariously*] I'll give her father blankets, tobacco... See.

JACK: [*sharply*] Don't be a fool, Brum. [*As a kylie shies past* BRUMBY] Tell the boys to let up, Wongana. He's drunk, can't you see? Mad drunk. They'll get the worst of it.

BRUMBY: [*shooting high and laughing*] Show 'em! Eh? [*As the women and children shrink together, crying out and wailing*] Show 'em who's boss, here...

JACK: Humour him or he'll shoot the lot of you. Let him have the girl, Wongana, for God's sake.

BRUMBY: [*pushing* WYLBA *out before him*] Come along now.

WYLBA: Wiah! Wiah!

She wails and moves off before him. The men surge after her threateningly. A kylie hits BRUMBY. *He shoots before him. There is a scream of pain.*

JACK: Get out. Get out, Brum. They'll do for you.
BRUMBY: [*laughing boisterously*] Do for me?

He goes off backwards, dragging and pushing WYLBA *with him.*

Do for me, eh? [*Shooting over the camp*] We'll see.

He goes off, shooting. Cries of fear and pain, the yells, screams and shouted imprecations of the blacks follow him.

END OF ACT ONE

ACT TWO

The kitchen of BRUMBY INNES' *homestead, a long room of mud bricks with brushwood screen for a verandah. We see the brushwood of the verandah, and its long sapling posts through a wide–open door. Windows on either side, double the size of ordinary windows and without glass, show level, sun–blasted country stretching to a far horizon under the glimmer of dawn. Stars are still in the sky; a butcher bird fluting. (Two notes on the musical pipes and a short chromatic, give it.) The light grows quickly to the full, clear radiance of early morning.*

BRUMBY *is asleep, snoring heavily, in a bunk below the fireplace, left. A box against the end of the bunk serves as a seat. A rifle leans to the wall near the hearth. There are shelves and tins for flour, tea, sugar, jam, in the corner on the other side of the fireplace; two smoke–blackened kerosene buckets for water on the hearth; and a bench for dishes and cooking pots under the window, left of the door. A table stands out from the window on the right, a chair at either end; a bottle of whisky and a quart pot are on the table. The door to the storeroom opens below the table on the right. A case of whisky has been pushed against the wall.* JACK CAREY, *stirring the ashes of the fire, raises his head to listen, stands poised, his arm hung as he was going to throw wood on the fire.* WYLBA, *curled in a faded pale blue gina–gina, is sleeping like a dog on the floor beside the table.*

WYLBA: [*wailing in her sleep*] Wiah! Wiah!
JACK: [*cursing under his breath*] Be quiet, can't you?

> *He throws a branch on the fire. As the flames leap up, he turns quickly to face the door.*

Who's there?

> POLLY, *a tall gin in a long, straight, dark blue gina–gina, standing against the doorpost, pressed close to it so as not to be seen in the light of the doorway, edges herself into the room, left of the door. She stares at* WYLBA, *at* BRUMBY *asleep on the bunk; then her eyes go to* JACK CAREY.

What is it, Polly?

POLLY: [*in flat, steady tones*] Boys comin'… bump him.

JACK: They are, are they?

POLLY: Eeh–erm.

JACK: What do they think they're goin' to do?

POLLY: Beat'm.

JACK: You wongie them not to be damn fools, Polly. You know Brumby… You know he doesn't care what he does when he's mad. He'll lay them all out soon as look at them.

POLLY: [*morosely*] Bin talkin' all time.

JACK: No good?

POLLY: No good. Boys mad too.

JACK: Wylba's Mickina's woman, isn't she?

POLLY: Father give'm Wylba when she baby.

WYLBA: [*stirring sleepily*] Mickina!

Waking, she looks about her.

JACK: He's her noova—lover, eh?

POLLY: Wylba… weary–booger noova.

JACK: She's got plenty of lovers? All the men in the camp want her?

POLLY: [*with a backward glance*] Boys comin'.

WYLBA: [*jumping up and running to the door, peering out excitedly*] Plenty boys… plenty sticks…

JACK: [*trying to wake* BRUMBY] Shake y'rself, Brum! [*Shaking him roughly*] Wake up. [*As there is no response from the heavy sleeper*] Wake up, you blasted idiot! [*To* POLLY] John Hallinan campin' Sixty Mile?

POLLY: Eeh–erm.

JACK: Sent a boy along to say he'd be over when they was musterin' the Sixty Mile, didn't he?

POLLY: Munga.

BRUMBY: What… wa'sh that?

JACK: Wake up. There's a mob comin' up from the camp to lay you out.

BRUMBY: Mob… what? Aw, go to hell!

He turns over to sleep again.

POLLY: [*looking from the doorway*] Horse trough, Jack.

WYLBA *withers away from her glance.*

JACK: [*pulling* BRUMBY *from the bunk*] How many?

WYLBA: [*excitedly*] Uloo... all men in camp.

She shrinks away under POLLY*'s glance.*

JACK: [*pitching* BRUMBY *to the floor*] Wake up, blast you! [*Kicking him*] I've a good mind to let you take what's comin' to you. [*Going to the table*] If we weren't the only two white men on the place...

He pours whisky into the quart pot.

BRUMBY: Wh'sh that...? What... Jack? What the bloody blazes...?

JACK: [*giving him the quart pot*] Here, put this into you.

He goes to the hearth, examines the rifle to see whether it is loaded, takes cartridges from a box on the shelf beside the fireplace, and puts them in his pocket.

BRUMBY: [*drinking*] That's the stuff! Good old Jack! [*As* JACK *puts the cartridges in his pocket*] What's up? What are you doin'?

JACK: Camp's comin' to lay you out. Pull y'self together. Can't y'hear 'em?

A distant murmur of voices is heard.

BRUMBY: Comin' to... lay me out? [*Struggling to his feet*] That's a good one. [*Laughing and fingering the revolver in his belt*] Comin' to...? [*His eyes wandering from* WYLBA *to* POLLY] Wylba... I *see*. And old Polly.

JACK goes to the door with the rifle in his hands, stands it against the doorpost and looks out. The natives are heard approaching with a noisy, clamorous chatter.

JACK: They're comin' round the wood heap, Brum.

BRUMBY: It's off with the old love and on with the new, Polly. [*To* WYLBA] Come here.

WYLBA: [*going to him cringingly, whining*] Wiah! Wiah!

BRUMBY: Stop that row!

He pushes her away roughly and with a kick, as all the natives from the camp swarm along the verandah, surge about the doorway and windows, the men in faded blue and yellow trousers, grey shirts, felt hats of station stockmen, with sticks and kylies in their hands.

JACK: Look out! Brum!

BRUMBY: [*startled and realising what he is up against, facing them harshly*] What the hell's got you, the lot of you? [*Roaring as he takes the revolver from his belt*] Take y'r carcases out of my daylight, or I'll shoot the whole damn lot of you.

The blacks hesitate to push on into the room.

JACK: [*in the doorway, using the butt of his rifle*] Keep back.

BRUMBY *takes aim, but his revolver clicks on an empty barrel.*

BRUMBY: [*snarling at* WYLBA] That's you, is it?

Pushing WYLBA *before him, he springs back into the storeroom and bangs the door.*

JACK: [*retreating as the blacks swarm forward*] Now's y'r chance! Clear out, the rest of you. He's got powder and shot to blow you to blazes in there.

A bullet cracks through a chink in the storeroom door. Most of the boys stampede for the open doorway. There is a howl of pain. All but MICKINA *retire to the verandah, frightened and cowed.*

WYLBA: [*screaming*] Mickina! Mickina!

MICKINA: [*dashing at the storeroom door*] Wylba!

BRUMBY: [*throwing back the door*] It's you, is it? [*Jeeringly*] Come on, Wylba, give Mick his spears.

The black springs at him.

WYLBA: [*dancing and screaming fiercely*] Munyinbunna, nuki–nuki, chungee–chungee.

As the black and BRUMBY *grapple and struggle,* JACK *holds the crowd in the doorway with his rifle, although they are more or less interested in the scrap.* BRUMBY *tries to use his revolver.*

Walyinna, booketera, kundikundi spa!

MICKINA *sets his teeth in the flesh of* BRUMBY'*s arm to make him drop the revolver.*

Belyee marl, chungee–chungee, belyee marl, koo.

BRUMBY *throws the black off from him and shoots.* MICKINA *falls.*

BRUMBY: [*gasping and blowing*] Have the police on to yer—the damn lot of yer, damn and blast yer. Clear out if yer don't want what Mick's got.

The boys drift out of sight from the windows and door.

WYLBA: [*wailing beside* MICKINA] Mickina! Mickina!

BRUMBY: [*running* WYLBA *into the store*] You stay where yer are put, blast yer!

He slams the storeroom door. JACK *goes to* MICKINA *and bends over him, feels his heart, examines his wound.*

JACK: He's all right. He'll come round. You've made a mess of this, Brum.

BRUMBY: [*sitting down and pouring himself some whisky*] Swine. Why didn't yer do for him, Polly? [*Drinking*] I gave yer the gun.

POLLY: [*in her slow, level tones*] Shoot'm… bin kangarooin'. Bullet go through hat… not hurt'm.

BRUMBY: [*surlily*] Got a charm against bullets, has he? Well, we'll see.

He takes the pipe and tobacco from his belt.

JACK: [*as the gin turns away*] Here, Polly, bring water.

She goes to the bench under the window, takes a tin dish and puts water in it from the buckets by the hearth, gives the dish to JACK *and returns to bucket; goes out for more water.* JACK *goes to the bunk, pulls a box from underneath and rummages in it for a piece of clean rag.*

BRUMBY: [*stuffing his pipe with tobacco*] I'll put the police on to'm for this.

JACK tears a strip of rag from the tail of a shirt and returns to MICKINA.

See if I don't. I'll damn well—

JACK: Y'll get more'n y'bargain for, if you do.

BRUMBY: What?

JACK: [*washing blood from the wound on the black's forehead*] Y'll get more'n you bargain for if you do.

BRUMBY: [*smoking*] How do yer make that out?

JACK: The boys'll talk about this girl—and you givin' old Polly there a gun to shoot Mick, first chance she got.

BRUMBY: They will, will they? Well let'm, I say. Let'm.

JACK: [*having tied a bandage around* MICKINA'*s head*] With this damned Morrison chap about—Protector of Aborigines, they call him—it'll go hard with yer.

BRUMBY: [*slowly, derisively*] Hard with *me*?

JACK: And there's John Hallinan, don't forget.

BRUMBY: What are yer givin' us?

JACK: If Morrison got onto it—the girl bein' under age.

BRUMBY: [*crowing hilariously*] A blasted nigger! What are yer givin' us? Ever heard of a white man doin' time for a black girl? Aw, go on...

JACK: But times is different, Brum. Times is changing. This Morrison chap—

BRUMBY: Changin' 'em, is he? Well, don't let him come pokin' his nose in, around here, that's all.

POLLY: [*in the doorway, a bucket of water on her head*] Bin comin'.

JACK: Who? Morrison?

> BRUMBY *goes to the door.*

BRUMBY: Looks like a couple of horses.

JACK: [*steering towards the door*] We don't want anybody around this mornin'. [*Peering under his hand*] John Hallinan's musterin' the Sixty Mile—

BRUMBY: It'll be him for a monte. Sent a boy over to say he'd be along when they was on the Sixty Mile, didn't he? I clean forgot.

JACK: He did.

BRUMBY: Eh, Polly. [*As she turns*] What the boys do with that bush mob we brought in yesterday?

POLLY: Yard'm.

JACK: You've been lucky, Brum, dead lucky. But you were bound to get caught one of these days. John Hallinan's stood a good deal from you, and he warned us, if the percentage of Nyedee calves went down this year, like it done last, along our boundary... he'd have to do something.

BRUMBY: Dry up, can't yer, [*going towards the black on the floor*] and help clean up this mess. Here, you, Polly, take Mickina down camp. [*As she stands staring down at the unconscious native*] Carry him on your back. You can, easy...

POLLY: [*flatly, looking down at the native who to her has a charmed life*] No.

BRUMBY: [*knowing her superstitions and that there is no time for argument*] Scared eh? [*To* JACK] Come on, then. We'll have to put him here.

JACK *helps to lift* MICKINA *and throw him on the bunk.*

Get a rag and wipe up that blood on the floor.

POLLY *goes to the bench under the window for rags while he throws water, from the dish on the floor, through the open door.* JACK *covers* MICKINA *with a grey blanket.*

JACK: It's more'n likely the boys will tell him about this.

POLLY *kneels with water and rags to clean the floor.*

BRUMBY: Tell him? [*In the doorway, looking out*] Tell him? I'll tell him meself. Ask him to send out the police. Hallinan's comin' in the top gate be the yards. He'll see them cleanskins, all right. Christ!

JACK: [*hobbling to the doorway*] What?

BRUMBY: He's got a woman with him.

JACK: A woman?

POLLY: [*looking up from the floor*] Bin campin' Sixty Mile.

BRUMBY: Been camping at the well with him, has she?

POLLY: [*finishing her job and going out with rags and bucket*] Eeh–erm.

JACK: His niece, May Hallinan, I suppose. Been stayin' on Nyedee for the winter.

BRUMBY, *falling back, passes a hand over his beard, gives his pants a hitch, and goes into the storeroom.* JACK *looks up.*

Gee, they're hitchin' their horses at the stable and walkin' over.

He glances anxiously at the native on the bunk, and returns to pull the blanket over him.

JOHN: [*calling*] Hullo! Anybody at home?

JACK: [*hurrying forward as* JOHN *and* MAY *appear in the doorway*] Mornin', John. Glad to see yer.

JOHN: [*coming into the room*] Morning, Jack. This is my niece, May Hallinan.

He is a man of middle age with greying hair, kind and sturdy, wearing well-washed white moleskins, pale blue shirt, wide-brimmed felt hat, leather belt with matchbox attached, pipe stuck through, stockwhip looped around his neck, and the elastic-sided boots of a stockman. MAY *is a pretty, shallow, city-bred girl, wearing riding breeches, a white blouse and stockman's wide-brimmed hat.*

MAY: Good morning, Mr. Carey. We *are* early birds, aren't we.

JACK: [*shaking hands with her, but standing so that she does not see the native on the bunk*] Not too early for this part of the world, miss.

MAY: It's nice riding before the sun gets too hot, isn't it?

JOHN: [*seeing the blood on the floor, but appearing not to while* MAY *is there*] How's the eyes, Jack?

JACK: [*cracking hardy, as always*] Good, thanks, John. They're real good. Though I can't see to read much, these days.

JOHN: Brumby about?

JACK: He... he's in the store.

BRUMBY *comes out, his hat on.*

BRUMBY: Gord a'mighty, John Hallinan, is it?

MAY: [*jauntily*] Hullo, Mr. Innes!

BRUMBY: Mornin', Miss May. Well, John, how's things?

JOHN: Not too bad, thanks, Brum.

MAY: [*hovering in the doorway, looking back over the plains*] Is that punti—that little yellow flower, on those bushes beside the verandah—Mr. Carey?

JACK: [*nervous and apologetic*] I don't know what yer call it.

BRUMBY: [*to* JOHN] Come on, sit down.

He goes to the table. JOHN *follows him.*

MAY: And that's desert pea, isn't it—the red out there?

JACK: The blacks call it murda–murda.

MAY: Oh, I *must* get some.

She goes out.

JOHN: [*before he sits down, staring at the native on the bunk*] Hullo? What's up?

JACK: Been havin' a dust–up with the boys, this mornin', John.

BRUMBY: Came to lay me out. So I let 'em have it.

JOHN: [*eyeing the stained floor*] Looks like it.

JACK: [*apologetically*] The natives is gettin' proper cheeky up here, John. You got to let'm have it now and again.

> *At this stage, the tempo quickens.* BRUMBY *is playing to keep* JOHN HALLINAN'*s attention off the native and avoid further explanation.*

BRUMBY: [*boisterously, holding up a nearly empty bottle of Black and White whisky*] Any of that whisky left, Jack? Got a case a couple of days ago [*as* JACK *goes to the case beside the storeroom door*] and old Jack's been boozin' up a bit. Never touched a woman in all his born days, he says, but he ain't so teetotal about sting.

> *He sits down.*

JACK: It's a lie.

BRUMBY: [*in good humour, making a butt of the old man*] He said that the other day when Ted Duffy was here. [*As* JACK *brings the bottle of whisky and puts it on the table*] Where's the tin opener? [*Finding a corkscrew on the table and going on to draw the cork*] Ted's camel–punching for Sparkes now, did yer know?

> JACK *brings another quart pot and a white enamelled mug from the bench to the table.*

Was through here with a load—

JOHN: [*as* BRUMBY *pours whisky into the enamelled mug*] Whoa!

BRUMBY: [*pushing the mug towards him*]…for Karrara. Havin' some Jack?

JACK: [*yielding to temptation*] Oh, well, just a drop.

BRUMBY: [*pouring and holding a pot out to* JACK] Been sixteen weeks on the road.

> *He pours for himself.* JACK *takes his pot and sits on a box out from the bunk.*

JOHN: No wonder Sparkes says loadin' for Karrara doesn't pay. He was just thirteen weeks late with our stores.

BRUMBY: [*drinking*] Well, here's skin off yer nose! [*Pouring for himself again*] Camels was stuck in the river. [*Pulling out his pipe and*

stoking it] But Sparko, he didn't worry. Went back to The Breakway
for a gutful. [*Holding the bottle to* JOHN] Come on, fill up.

JOHN: No, thanks. How about some water?

BRUMBY: Spoilin' the good stuff. Eh, Polly? When he was here, Ted
was sayin', too, he had to chase the bloomin' camels every morning
after they'd camped. And it takes him a day and a half to git 'em
again. [*Shouting*] Eh, Polly!

> POLLY *appears in the doorway.*

Water.

> POLLY *moves in a leisurely, dignified fashion to the bench under
> the window, takes an enamelled jug, dips it into a bucket on the
> hearth.*

Well, when Ted was here, couple of weeks ago, Ted and me—

JOHN: [*as* POLLY *puts the jug of water beside him*] Thank you, Polly.

> *He pours water into his mug and she goes out again.*

BRUMBY: We got onto young Tommy, the half–caste [*winking at* JOHN]
to tell us who his father was…

JACK: Aw… dry up.

BRUMBY: And who'd you think he said? [*Roaring with laughter*] And
who do yer think young Tommy said was his father? Why, Jack…
old Jack Carey!

JACK: It's a lie, John. Him and Ted got drinkin' together and put the
kid up to it.

BRUMBY: [*mimicking* JACK] Never touched a native woman in me
life…

JOHN: There's not many men have knocked about the Nor'–west as
long as you have, can say that, Jack.

JACK: But you know it's true?

JOHN: I believe you, Jack.

> MAY *comes in from the verandah with red and yellow flowers in
> her hand.*

BRUMBY: Thousands wouldn't.

MAY: Believe what?

JACK: [*in an agony*] Aw, dry up.

MAY: [*as the men move to give her a chair*] Don't move, I'll sit here.

She perches herself on the bench before the window and looks curiously about her.

BRUMBY: Why, that… [*Relishing the fear and discomfort of the other men that he will repeat what he has said*] It's going to rain, Miss May.

MAY: [*fanning herself vigorously with her hat*] Does it ever rain up here? Oh!

She jumps down and goes to look at the boy on the bunk.

Somebody sick?

JACK: [*awkwardly*] One of the boys. An… accident, miss.

BRUMBY: [*dryly*] He got hurt.

JACK: [*to divert* MAY'*s attention*] She'd like some tea, perhaps, Brum?

MAY: [*in her affected, sprightly way*] I'd love it!

BRUMBY: [*shouting*] Polly!

MAY: [*returning to her seat on the bench*] I've got what you'd call a forty horsepower thirst, Mr. Innes.

BRUMBY: [*jocosely*] Hundred and forty's nearer my mark. [*As* POLLY *comes into the doorway*] Tea for the lady, Polly.

POLLY: [*stately and indifferent, eyeing the girl*] Eeh–ermm.

She comes and goes from the bench to the fireplace, making tea.

BRUMBY: [*returning to the table and whisky bottle*] Yer see…

JOHN: [*refusing whisky*] No. No, thank you, Brum. Fact of the matter, what I came to see you about—

WYLBA, *offstage, screeches and wails.*

BRUMBY: He… old Jack rules the roost here, Miss May. Head stockman and all of that. And if he says—

MAY: [*hearing* WYLBA *wailing*] What's that?

BRUMBY: If he says it's going to rain, well, it's going to rain.

JACK: [*growling*] Head stockman, be blowed.

BRUMBY: [*sitting on the end of the table*] Head stockman! [*Throwing off another whisky*] Gord a'mighty, what am I thinkin' of? And him a bleedin' landowner like the rest of us. Wanted to sell me his place: homestead, a rusty tank, bush shed and a hundred horses. Leastways, he thought there was a hundred horses.

JOHN: More like two hundred, I reck'n, Jack.

BRUMBY: For a hundred pounds... goin'... goin'...

MAY: [*as* POLLY *puts a cup of tea beside her*] Thank you.

BRUMBY: Gone! 'No thank you, Jack,' I says. 'I got all the horses I want: and if I want more—I can always *get 'em.*'

JACK: You mustered'm for me in 1915, remember, John?

JOHN: I remember all right, Jack.

BRUMBY: Ten years ago.

JOHN: [*chuckling*] 'They're quiet,' he says. 'They're fairly quiet. I've mustered 'em meself.' He might've done, down a kind of gutter between the hills, there was, over at his place...

MAY: [*putting down her cup and coming forward to listen*] Nyedee hills, Unc, that range at the back of the run?

JOHN: [*nodding*] Steep as the back of your hand, all tussocky spinifex and wash–aways. Well, we went after 'em. Got a hundred and twenty, wild as hawks; eight and ten year old, not branded. 'Not branded, Jack,' I says. 'Oh yes, they're branded,' he says. 'Can't see the brand,' I says. 'Oh well, I branded 'em all right,' he says: 'through the fence, and the brand might've got cold.'

> *Laughter.*

BRUMBY: [*when the laughter has subsided*] Thought he was all–in, the night he come ridin' up to the stockyards on his old blind horse.

JACK: [*gruffly*] Best night horse in the Nor'–west.

JOHN: Old Hero, Jack?

JACK: Yes.

JOHN: Flintlock, out of Reflection. He was a good horse all right, Jack.

BRUMBY: Well, y'r never see such a pair of scrags, the night they come in. Been livin' on salt emu, or somethin'. The old horse could jest about set one foot in front of the other and Jack here, was swayin' about and singin'...

JOHN: [*chuckling*] Same old song? [*Singing*] 'So it's shift boys, shift. There isn't the slightest doubt...'

BRUMBY: That's right.

JACK: [*apologetically*] Touch of the sun... and the diarrhoea or somethin'.

JOHN: Why didn't you come to me, Jack?

JACK: Oh, well, you're a family man now, John. The women don't like an old moocher knockin' about.

JOHN: Women be damned. We were real sore on Nyedee when we found you'd come here.

MAY: [*prowling around and posing for* BRUMBY, *who is watching her*] What a lovely big kitchen.

POLLY *goes to the bench for a cup and saucer.*

JOHN: Funny thing, too. I got a feeling something was wrong with you.

BRUMBY: Eeh–erm?

JOHN: Went out to bring you in, and found your tracks comin' here.

JACK: [*apologetically*] Must've been pretty crook, John. Don't know rightly what happened. It was thirty miles against sixty, I suppose, and the old horse just took the nearest track.

JOHN: Oh well, there's always a home for you on Nyedee, Jack.

BRUMBY: [*boisterously*] Here, what are you up to, John Hallinan? Not takin' me right–hand man from me, are yer?

JACK: I can be a bit of use here, John… look after things when Brum's out musterin'… or on the skoot.

BRUMBY: [*uproariously*] My oath, he can. Hides the whisky and sees the gins don't pinch all the tea and sugar. Hear about that last mob we was takin' down?

JOHN: No.

BRUMBY: Gord, we had a time with them. Jack was comin' along to cook for us, and first night out, the mob broke. Dark? It was that dark, y'couldn't hear a dog bark; and away the blasted brutes went. We chased 'em for a couple of hours. Brought 'em back to camp. And away they went agen. Next night it was the same. Cockeyed Bob, and a half–caste woman he had with him, was to do a go on night watch. They was changing horses with young Tommy and Mickina when the cattle made off. Bob waited for Tommy to go after'm and Tommy waited for Bob. The woman didn't know what to do and galloped after'm on her own.

JOHN: If the bullocks start breakin' like that, they make a habit of it.

BRUMBY: Third night, the boys fell off their horses and went to sleep where they fell. There was no gettin' a move out of any of 'em. I was dead to the world meself.

JOHN: But you got a bit of sleep during the day.

BRUMBY: We did, off and on, but the b—'s [*Looking at* MAY] beasts was wild as flies. There they was, moochin' along, quiet enough, and there's me, havin' a bit of a snooze in the shade... and away they go.

JACK: Bad as that mob we brought down from Nyedee—an' lost about half. Remember, John?

JOHN: Too right I remember, Jack.

BRUMBY: Third night, when I lay down, them bullocks could've broke to kingdom come. But Jack thought he was the on'y man to be trusted with'm. Went on, ridin' round'm all night—a blind man on a blind horse, singin'...

JOHN: [*singing*] 'For it's shift, boys, shift...'

BRUMBY: That's right. And he held'm on his own. Beasts must've knowed his voice.

JACK: They was dead–beat—like the rest of yer.

JOHN: Good old Jack!

BRUMBY: Best all–round stockman in the Nor'–west.

JOHN: Haven't I always said so, Jack?

MAY: Oh, do sing that song, Mr. Carey! I'd love to hear you.

JACK: [*shaking his head*] Got no voice, now.

BRUMBY: Can't sing 'less he's well oiled, Miss May, [*pouring whisky into a quart pot*] or ridin' round the cattle.

    He hands the quart pot to JACK.

JOHN: Come on, Jack. Just one verse. There's no one can sing 'The Old Jig Jog' like you. [*Tuning up*] 'I'm travellin' along the Castlereagh, for I'm a station hand...'

BRUMBY: [*joining in*] 'I'm handy with the roping pole, I'm handy with the brand...'

    JACK, *having drunk the whisky, puts down the pot and sings, diffidently at first, then with all the spirit of a stockman who thinks his game the finest on earth.*

JACK: For I can ride a rowdy colt, or swing an axe all day,
          But there's no demand for station hands along the Castlereagh.
          So it's shift boys, shift, there isn't the slightest doubt,

    JOHN *and* BRUMBY *join in the chorus:*

    We've got to make a move for the stations further out.

With the pack horse running after, for he follows like a dog,
We get over lots of country at the old jig jog.

JOHN: Next verse. Come on, Jack, 'Now you see this black horse…'

MAY: Go on, Mr. Carey, please!

JACK: [*singing*]

Now, you see this old black horse I ride, if you notice what's
    his brand,
He wears a crooked R, you see, no better in the land,
He takes a lot of beating, and the other day we tried,
For a bit of a joke, with a racing bloke, for twenty quid a side.

And it was shift, boys, shift, for there wasn't the slightest
    doubt,
I had to make him shift, for the money was nearly out.
But I cantered home a winner with the other at the flog,
He's a red–hot sort of pick–up with the old jig jog.

I asked a cove for shearin' once, along the Marthaga,
'We shear non–Union here,' says he. 'I call it scab,' says I.
I looked along the shearin' floor before I turned to go,
There was eight, or ten, damned Chinamen, ashearin' in a
    row.

So it's shift, boys, shift, there isn't the slightest doubt,
I had to make a shift with the leprosy about.
So I saddled up me horses and I whistled to me dog,
And I left his scabby station at the old jig jog.

I went to Illawarra where the brother keeps a farm,
They have to ask the landlord's leave before they lift their
    arm.
The landlord owns the countryside, man, woman, dog and
    cat,
And they haven't the cheek to dare to speak without they
    touch their hat.

The black on the bunk has been stirring during the singing and
WYLBA *is heard wailing in the store.*

So it's shift, boys, shift, there isn't the slightest doubt,
Their little landlord god and I would soon have fallen out,
Was I to touch me hat to him? Was I his bloomin' dog?
So I hooks–up for the country at the old jig jog.

WYLBA: [*crying in the storeroom, her voice rising above the singing*]
Walygee booger! Walygee booger!

MAY: What's that?

WYLBA: [*her voice rising to a scream of imprecation as she bangs on
the door*] Munyin–bunna, nunki–nunki. Chungee–chungee!

BRUMBY: [*pouring himself another drink*] Eh?

WYLBA: [*continuing her tune of rage and despair*] Walyina, booketera,
kundi–kundi, spa!

BRUMBY: [*maliciously, as he drinks*] Oh that! That's one of old Polly's
kids. [*Jerking his head towards* POLLY, *who is washing and putting
away tea things at the bench under the window*] She shut her up in
the store—for stealing the sugar, or something...

WYLBA: Chungee–chungee, belyee marl, koo!

POLLY: [*slowly and clearly, facing* BRUMBY, *her voice flat, without
emotion*] Liar.

JOHN: [*uneasily, sensing domestic disturbances, and anxious for his
niece not to discover them*] Well, we better get down to tin tacks,
Brumby. Fact of the matter is, I didn't mean this to be... a polite
morning call.

BRUMBY: [*derisively*] Go on? [*Tipping the bottle again*] Have another
drink?

JOHN: [*firmly and sternly*] Fact of the matter is, we've got to come to
some understanding about what's happening...

BRUMBY: [*guilelessly, as* JOHN *does not take the proffered pot, drinking
himself*] Jesus. What's happening?

JOHN: The percentage of our calves, this end of the run, is much less
than anywhere else. The feed's good; there are more wells. And at
the figure you're showin', your cows must be havin' two and three
calves a year.

BRUMBY: [*crowing derisively*] I ain't responsible for the actions of my
cows.

JOHN: There's the branded calf you had in your yards the other day
when Munga was over. And the mother was one of our cows.

BRUMBY: [*laughing as though over a good joke*] Cripes... and you should have heard him go off!

WYLBA *wails more quietly now.*

JOHN: I did.

BRUMBY: Well, what are you goin' to do about it?

JOHN: [*amazed*] Do about it?

BRUMBY: [*flatly*] Do about it.

JOHN: You'll see what I'm goin' to do about it.

MICKINA *on the bunk lifts himself, listens to* WYLBA *still wailing in the store, lies looking warily around, then listens with closed eyes.*

It's over the fence, Brum, the way you been carrying on. Way you been treating Nyedee. I've shut my eyes to it, over and over again. And I've warned you...

BRUMBY: [*jocosely*] He's warned me, Jack!

JOHN: So as not to make any bad feeling between us. But it's come to this. Things can't go on the way they're doing. The run won't stand it. We lost 4,000 bullocks out of 12,000 in the drought...

JACK: [*with grudging admiration*] Nyedee lost less than most.

JOHN: Why? Wasn't it because I worked night and day moving the cattle. Wherever there was a bit of feed or water, we moved. Kept movin' 'em.

JACK: That's right. You did, John. I'm not sayin' you don't deserve anything you got. You do. But Brum—he jest can't run straight.

BRUMBY: [*watching* MAY, *who is trying the storeroom door*] Speak for y'r self!

MICKINA: [*raising himself cautiously and making a dash for the door*] All time... branding your calves, John!

BRUMBY: [*starting to his feet, hand on his revolver*] God damn and blast—

MICKINA: [*in the doorway*] Bring in cleanskin. He say brand'm B.1.4.

MICKINA *vanishes.*

BRUMBY: These bloody niggers is gettin' too bloody cheeky.

JOHN: He's about right, I reckon, Brum. It's only what I've heard before. Anyway, it's got to stop. I give you fair warning. I'm watching you

from now on and if I find you running in any more Nyedee calves,
I'll have the law on you.

BRUMBY: [*gazing at* MAY] Law? There ain't any law—out here.

MAY: [*provocatively*] Except for abos.

BRUMBY: What's that?

MAY: Didn't I hear you say you'd have the mounted police to your
boys?

BRUMBY: That's right.

> *There is a stir of movement: muffled laughter outside.*

What's that?

JOHN: What?

JACK: [*going to the door*] Who's there?

> *Natives jump up behind the windows and run past the door,
> laughing and hooting.*

BRUMBY: Well, I'm damned.

WYLBA: [*springing into the doorway, flanked by* MICKINA *and other boys,
yelling, hooting their anger and laughter*] Minyin bunna nunki–nunki,
chungee–chungee, walyina, booketera, kundi–kundi, spa.

> JACK *goes to the door.*

Dirty dog… koo!

> *She, and all the blacks, disappear on this last note of mockery
> and defiance.*

BRUMBY: [*striding to the door*] By God, if I don't—

JOHN: [*harshly*] Hold on, Brumby. You might wait till we're gone.

JACK: [*from the door of the storeroom*] They've broke a hole in the
wall, helped themselves to tobacco. There's flour and sugar all over
the place.

BRUMBY: [*swinging to the storeroom*] Broken in, have they? If I don't
make some of'm sweat for this.

> *He goes into the store.*

JACK: [*to* JOHN] Wylba must've been grubbin' a hole through, and the
boys was helping her from the outside, all the time she was yellin'.

JOHN: Quite likely.

MAY: [*lightly*] An interesting morning, Unc!

JOHN: Glad you like it.

MAY: [*lightly*] I'd no idea life could be so exciting outback, these days. What a good thing I made you bring me with you this morning. Mr. Innes is quite a thrill, isn't he?

JOHN: [*uneasily*] It's all very well, May, to trot out your little airs and graces for men like Cecil Grey or Arthur Leigh; but Brum's different...

MAY: Different?

JOHN: He wouldn't understand... flirting.

MAY: [*laughing*] Not understand? Oh, Unc, you're priceless! Why he took to it like a duck to water when we met him over at Koodgieda, last month.

JOHN: [*as* POLLY *stands beside him, erect and dignified*] What's up, Polly?

POLLY: Go longa, Nyedee, John.

JOHN: Why? What's up, Polly?

POLLY: Go Nyedee, with you, John.

JOHN: [*puzzled*] Go to Nyedee with me, Polly?

POLLY: Good house–girl sweep, sew, make bread, tea... wash'm [*with a gesture over herself*] all time.

JOHN: Why? Had a row with Brumby, Polly?

POLLY: Bita muna, Brumby.

JOHN: Fed up with him, are you?

POLLY: Eeh–erm. Fed up.

JOHN: But you've been with Brumby, how many years?

POLLY: Weary booger years. Tell me get out now. Want young woman. Pretty young girl... Wylba. [*Looking at* MAY] Two women, maybe.

JOHN: Oh, that's it, is it? He wants a young and pretty woman, now... two women, perhaps.

BRUMBY: [*coming from the storeroom with* JACK *behind him*] Taken all they wanted: tobacco, pipes, jam, sugar, flour, tea. Niggers on this station need a lesson. That's what they need. I'll ride into Yanigee with you, John, and get the police on to this.

JACK: Aw... go on, Brum. There's not much damage done. We got plenty of stuff till next loading. Tell him not to be a fool, John.

BRUMBY: I'm goin' for the police, I tell yer. Think I'm goin' to stand for niggers raidin' the store?

JOHN: You'll be making the mistake of your life, if you go dragging the police into your affairs with natives, Brum.

BRUMBY: [*propitiatingly*] Cut it out, John. Cut it out. White men's got to stand together or there'll be no livin' in the Nor'–west. I'm no bloody angel—but you ain't, y'rself. And where cattle's concerned it's fifty–fifty.

JOHN: [*harshly*] Speak for yourself.

BRUMBY: Oh, well, they're doin' a bit of brandin' all round yer, and if y'don't do it, more fool you. You can't tell me if Three Hills, or Karrara, had a killer in the yards, and you rode up, unexpected, you'd care to go down to the stockyards.

JOHN: That's not the question.

BRUMBY: Oh, well, the long and the short of it is, John, if there's been a mistake about any of your calves…

JOHN: There's been mistakes about a good many of our calves, Brum.

BRUMBY: [*amiably*] Oh, well, if there has, there has, John. But cut it out… cut it out, for Gord's sake… and I'll make 'em up to you. I want to stand well with you. You been square with me… dead square… and, by Christ… I'll deal square with you.

JOHN: [*dryly*] Pleased to hear it.

BRUMBY: There's a bush mob in the yards now. You can go and take y'r pick.

JACK: Or else [*glancing towards* BRUMBY *for affirmation*] the boys'll be musterin' fats, next moon, John, if y'cared to come over then…

BRUMBY: Anything in reason, so long as we cut out the square talk and stop jawrin'. [*Cunningly, his eyes following* MAY*'s every movement*] But I'd go while the goin's good, if I was you, John. I might change me mind. Feelin' real good, this mornin'. Lovin' me neighbour like meself. But it mightn't last, might it, Jack?

JACK: Too right, it mightn't.

BRUMBY: You go along with him, Jack. See he don't skin me while I fix up me tucker bags for goin' into Yanigee.

JOHN: Right. [*Going to the door*] Coming, May?

MAY: [*hesitating, glancing back at* BRUMBY, *who is busy folding and rolling his groundsheet and blanket on the floor*] It'll be dusty up at the yards—I may as well wait here.

JACK: [*standing in the doorway*] What?

He looks anxiously at BRUMBY *who appears occupied with his pack.*

JOHN: We'll be back in two–twos.

JACK *jams on his hat. He and* JOHN *turn away.*

BRUMBY: [*genially, calling after them*] See you fix him all right, Jack. Jack'll see you get a fair deal, John. Thinks there's no one like you. And it'd break me heart to see the way the brands on some of them beasts has been mugged.

MAY, *standing in the doorway, watches* JOHN *and* JACK *go to the stockyards; then turns to look at* BRUMBY, *who goes up to the bench under the window for his tucker bags of unbleached calico, and spreads them out, apparently oblivious but intensely conscious of her all the time.*

MAY: [*flirtatiously*] Well, I came, didn't I?

BRUMBY: [*not looking at her, and going on with his preparations*] Warned you not to.

MAY: [*gaily*] That's why I came, of course.

BRUMBY: [*taking tins down from the shelf beside the hearth*] I said… if you came to see me… you'd stay.

MAY: [*teasing him*] But I didn't come to see you, Mr. Innes. I came to see… Mr. Carey.

BRUMBY: [*as if talking to himself, and reaching for another tin*] White women are scarce. We got to get 'em as best we can.

MAY *takes a powder box with mirror and lipstick, tied up in a handkerchief, from her breeches pocket, powders her face daintily and reddens her lips.* BRUMBY *watches her.*

Gord A'mighty!

MAY: Why…

She laughs, pleased to have attracted his attention.

BRUMBY: What are you doin' that for?

MAY: Oh… habit, I suppose. When in doubt, powder your nose.

BRUMBY, *continuing his packing, rolls a huge piece of salt meat in a bag, pours flour into a bag, and throws them over to the pack.*

BRUMBY: Where's the tea?

He finds it and pours tea into a bag, spilling some, takes a tin of jam and goes to the pack, kneels down to arrange the bundles.

MAY: [*coming nearer and sitting on the end of the table to watch him*] I'm going down south on Saturday, you know. Uncle and Cecil Grant are taking me into Yanigee. We're camping two nights on the road. I adore camping, don't you?

BRUMBY *grunts.*

And then I'm to be married next month, you know. Didn't you know? Oh… I thought everybody knew.

BRUMBY *rises, goes to shelf for some cartridges and reloads his revolver.* MAY *is alarmed.*

What are you doing that for?

BRUMBY: You never can tell when it may be useful.

MAY: But I thought the abos up here were all so quiet?

BRUMBY: They are. But sometimes one gets over the fence; or a sulky fellow comes in from the bush.

He thrusts the revolver into the leather case on his belt, and goes to the bench again. Pouring sugar into a tucker bag, he spills a good deal.

MAY: [*going towards him*] Here, you're spilling it all. I'll hold the bag for you.

BRUMBY *pours the sugar as she holds the bag, staring at her, with glowering fascination.*

BRUMBY: [*almost in a whisper*] I want you.

He drops the sugar tin.

MAY: [*startled*] What? What did you say?

BRUMBY: [*moving between her and the door*] You're like water on a dry stretch to a thirsty man.

MAY: [*scared*] Oh—

BRUMBY: They call me the brumby.

MAY: [*frightened but fencing*] I've heard what a wonderful bushman you are.

BRUMBY: You have, have you? [*With easy conceit*] Well, that's right.

I've knocked round with gins all me days: gins and bullocks, blacks
and brumbies. Born in the Breakway Country. Never been to school.
But I want a white woman. How about stayin' here?

MAY: [*coquettishly, thinking she has the reins again*] It's awfully sweet
of you to ask me, but—

BRUMBY: [*throwing an arm around her and holding her*] You been
foolin' all the men you've set eyes on up here, for the last six
months. You aren't goin' to fool me.

MAY: Let me go.

BRUMBY: [*laughing*] Not on your life.

MAY: If you don't…

BRUMBY: Well?

MAY: I'll scream the place down.

BRUMBY: Scream away. They wouldn't hear you at the yards… even
if I let you.

MAY: [*struggling, but yielding*] Oh you…

BRUMBY: [*laughing triumphantly and embracing her roughly, as he
pushes her towards the bunk*] I like 'em thoroughbred and buckin'
a bit at first.

END OF ACT TWO

ACT THREE

The kitchen of BRUMBY INNES' *homestead, four or five months later. It looks the same as ACT TWO except that there is a gramophone on the table and a jar of yellow wildflowers. A few brightly coloured magazines lie about; a girl's wide–leafed straw hat with a ribbon hangs from the knob of a chair; and a chintz umbrella and tennis racquet lean beside the doorpost; a scarlet kimono dangles from a peg over the bunk. There is a bookcase beside the storeroom door.*

MAY, *in a yellow frock, is leaning against the doorpost, right, and gazing out over the plains.*

POLLY *passes the window on the left, a bucket of water on her head; in the doorway she pauses, lifts the bucket down, and moves with slow dignity to the fireplace, puts the bucket against the wall, stirs the ashes of the fire, and throws wood on.*

MAY: Does anything ever happen? Does anyone ever come, Polly?

POLLY: Eeh–erm.

MAY: Do they?

POLLY: Eeh–erm.

MAY: [*after a long silence in which* POLLY *washes some dishes at the bench under the window*] How long have I been here, watching the road… every dust? [*Bitterly*] Weary booger years? [*As* POLLY *does not answer, continuing very slowly to dip and dry cups and saucers*] Polly!

POLLY: [*mildly, with surprise at the sharpness of her voice*] Eeh–erm.

MAY: How long have I been here?

POLLY: Two moon, maybe.

MAY: Two months… it's a dream, surely. Some queer sort of dream I'm in. It feels just like that, Polly. You know how you can't move in a dream; the red dust blows into you—columns of it. Winning–arras, isn't it you call them, the whirlwinds?

POLLY: Eeh–erm.

MAY: It's got into my brain… the red dust. I've been eating it. It's suffocating me. [*Whirling away from the door and walking up and down*] If only I could do something. What can I do, Polly?

POLLY: [*indifferently, glancing contemptuously and moving off with the two blackened kerosene buckets*] Murndoo.

MAY: [*hysterically*] Murndoo. Don't know. You don't know. I don't know. And there's nobody else to know. [*Desperately*] Is Jack Carey back yet?

POLLY: [*imperturbably*] Fetch'm killer.

MAY: When will *he* be back?

POLLY: Brumby?

MAY: Yes.

POLLY: [*flatly*] Murndoo.

MAY: [*despairingly*] Don't know. You don't know anything I ask you. And the rest of the camp's gone pink–eye, till Brumby gets back. And the boys the police took. Will they come back? Mickina and the boys, I mean. Cockeyed Bob, Bungarra and the rest of them?

POLLY: [*staring away over the plains*] Murndoo.

MAY: [*petulantly*] Murndoo! Murndoo! Don't say that to me again. You're not to say you don't know to me again. Do you hear?

> POLLY *stalks off, a bucket on her head.*

Damn you.

> *When* POLLY *has disappeared, a low wailing and groaning is heard.*

Who's there?

> *The tall, stooping figure of an old native woman appears outside, coming from the left. Her dark blue dungaree gina–gina is almost black with grease and dirt. A dust–coloured rag, once white, is bound over her eyes and around her head. She walks with a stick, groping with one thin, scrawny arm before her, in the way of the blind.*

TULLAMURRA: [*hovering in the doorway*] Tullamurra.

MAY: Tullamurra. The blind one.

TULLAMURRA: [*wailing*] Ai–ey! Ai–ey!

MAY: [*going to her*] Poor old thing! How are the eyes, this afternoon?

TULLAMURRA: [*rocking herself in agony*] Ai–ey!

MAY: Poor old Tullamurra! Want some drops in them?

TULLAMURRA: [*hopefully*] Eeh–erm?

MAY: Very well.

She goes to the bookcase near the storeroom door for a bottle of eye–lotion, while TULLAMURRA *sinks down on the floor and stretches flat on her back.*

Gargoyle. That's it.

Taking the bottle, she goes to the bench for a teaspoon.

It's the black drops are the best, isn't it, Tullamurra?

TULLAMURRA: [*writhing and squirming*] Ai–ey!

MAY, *kneeling down beside her, pours black lotion from the bottle into the teaspoon; the old woman pushes back her bandage.*

MAY: Oh, they do look bad! Hold your eyelids apart.

She drops the lotion from the spoon into the old woman's eyes.

TULLAMURRA: Ai–ey!

MAY: [*rising, bottle and spoon in her hand*] There… it hurts! But it will do them good.

TULLAMURRA: [*writhing and squirming on the floor like a worm stabbed with a fork*] Ai–ey! Ai–ey!

MAY, *after putting the bottle and spoon on the bench, takes the chair at the end of the table, sits down and watches as* TULLAMURRA *tries to sit up, holding her eyes and moaning with pain.*

MAY: Stay where you are, Tullamurra.

TULLAMURRA: [*gratefully*] Eeh–erm.

MAY *goes to the door and stares out, then returns to the chair as* TULLAMURRA *sits up.*

MAY: That better?

TULLAMURRA: Eeh–erm.

MAY: What's this row between Brumby and the camp about, Tullamurra? Now don't you say, 'Murndoo'. You do know. And if you don't tell me, I won't do your eyes anymore. [*As* TULLAMURRA *moves her head to listen whether* POLLY *is about*] No. Polly's over at the well.

TULLAMURRA: Brumby shoot over camp.

MAY: I know that. But why? Why did he shoot over the camp, Tullamurra?

TULLAMURRA: Blackfellow badgee.

MAY: Cross, eh? Angry with Brumby?

TULLAMURRA: Eeh–erm. Boys come up… plenty sticks… beat'm.

MAY: But they shouldn't have done that. Should they?

TULLAMURRA: [*firing up*] Brumby take'm Wylba. Bring Wylba [*gesturing about her*] yere.

MAY: What?

TULLAMURRA: [*emphatically*] Brumby shoot over camp. Take Wylba.

MAY: He had no right to shoot over the camp and take Wylba. That was it, was it?

TULLAMURRA: [*fearfully*] Eeh–erm. [*Listening for* POLLY] Yienda not telling Brumby?

MAY: No. I won't tell him. Wylba is very young, isn't she, Tullamurra?

TULLAMURRA: Eeh–erm. Mickina tell Morrison.

MAY: The Protector of Aborigines. That's why Wylba had to go down to Yanigee with him, and Uncle John… That's why they wouldn't let me go.

POLLY: [*coming in with water, one bucket on her head, the other in her hand, yelling furiously when she sees* TULLAMURRA] What you bin sayin'? [*Threatening her*] Get out!

TULLAMURRA: [*scrambling to her feet*] Wiah! Wiah!

MAY: What is it? What's the matter?

POLLY: [*marching to the fireplace*] Tell'm get the hell out of here.

MAY: [*furiously*] Stay where you are, Tullamurra. I'll give orders in my own house, Polly. [*As* TULLAMURRA, *wailing and holding out her hands blindly, moves towards the door*] Wait a minute, Tullamurra. I'll get you some tobacco.

> *She goes to the bookcase, takes a plug from a box while* TULLAMURRA *wavers deprecatingly and* POLLY *fixes her with a gaze of sombre will power.*

There!

> *She gives the tobacco, at which the old woman beams, and turns to go, without thanks, as is the native fashion. She stumbles at the door, groping her way with hands before her.* POLLY *follows her out. They are heard jabbering outside, their voices shrill and quarrelsome. Another native woman turns around the doorpost*

on the right, with an eye cocked to be sure POLLY *has not seen her. She is of average height, fat and jolly looking, in a tawny, dust–coloured skirt, man's hat and coat.*

Oh, it's you, Warrarie! What do you want?

WARRARIE: [*ingratiatingly*] Got'm t'read, missus?

MAY: What for… you want thread, Warrarie?

WARRARIE: [*turning and showing brown limbs through a very torn skirt*] Weary booger, dress.

MAY: [*laughing*] I should think so.

WARRARIE: Poor booger me. [*Wheedlingly*] Got'm gina–gina store miah, meetchie?

MAY: A new dress? What on earth do you want a new gina–gina for?

WARRARIE: [*gurgling, coy and sly, hugging herself*] Got'm noova.

MAY: Noova… a lover?

WARRARIE: Eeh–erm.

MAY: But your husband's only dead a few months. Isn't that his hat and coat you're wearing?

WARRARIE: [*unabashed*] Eeh–erm.

MAY: Where you get'm lover?

WARRARIE: [*giggling and cuddling herself delightedly*] Bullock muster… Nyedee… Young man… strong feller.

MAY: Munga?

WARRARIE: [*gurgling happily*] Eeh–erm.

MAY: Poor booger me. Got no lover, Warrarie.

WARRARIE: Eeh? [*Chancing an upsquint and owl's eye, as if to say 'What are you giving us?'*] Wiah?

MAY: Only Brumby.

WARRARIE: [*confidentially, leaning forward*] Yienda, kurrie… go bullock muster.

MAY: [*laughing*] A pretty young woman, am I? [*Thoughtfully*] Tell you what, Warrarie. We run away, you and I. We go bush… find lover for me?

WARRARIE: [*flatly and with emphasis*] No!… Brumby chase'm… beat'm… break'm back… kick'm be'ind.

POLLY: [*coming in, threateningly*] Go, woodheap, you!

MAY: [*jumping down from the table excitedly*] Mind your own business, Polly. Don't dare to chase her away while I'm talking to her.

POLLY: [*going to the fireplace, scowling and muttering*] Brumby tell'm.

MAY: Well, I won't have you interfering with me. Do you understand?

POLLY: [*waving her hand towards the horizon*] Bin comin'…

MAY: Coming? [*Going to the door*] Who?

WARRARIE: [*looking out beside her*] John Hallinan, may be.

MAY: Oh! [*With excitement*] There's Jack Carey! Who is it, Mr. Carey?

JACK: [*passing the window*] What?

MAY: There's someone coming, the gins say. That dust over there.

> POLLY *comes to the door behind* WARRARIE.

JACK: [*his hand on his heart, walking crookedly, with a limp*] Who is it, Polly?

POLLY: John Hallinan's buggy.

MAY: Uncle John?

JACK: Brumby ridin'?

WARRARIE: Boys ridin'?

POLLY: Brumby in buggy, may be.

MAY: I'll go down to the gate to meet them.

WARRARIE: [*wheedlingly*] Got'm little feller new dress, meetchie?

MAY: Oh, I forgot. [*Coming back into the room*] Where are the keys, Polly? I see.

> *She goes to the bookcase, takes the keys from the shelf, and fits a key in the storeroom door.*

Just wait a minute, Warrarie.

> *She goes into the storeroom.*

POLLY: [*to* JACK, *growling*] Give gina–gina.

JACK: [*letting himself down carefully onto the chair on the far side of the table*] Lazy old swob! Better not let Brumby catch you, hanging round cadgin' gina–ginas. You can go up and help them kill and skin that beast anyhow, Warrarie.

WARRARIE: [*watching* MAY *with eager delight as she comes from the storeroom, a piece of red print in her hands*] Yukk–eye!

> MAY, *after locking the door and hanging the keys on their peg, gives the material to* WARRARIE.

MAY: There you are.

WARRARIE, *snatching it away, gurgles ecstatically, fondling the stuff.*

WARRARIE: Pretty… pretty gina–gina.

She slides out.

JACK: [*calling after her*] See you don't let the stomach gas into that beast!

MAY: [*going to the door*] Are you sure it's Uncle John, Polly? I can't see anything but dust.

POLLY: Eeh–erm.

MAY: [*turning to* JACK CAREY] I begged Uncle to come and take me back with him, Mr. Carey—[*As he sits, bowed with pain, over the table*] Are you all right?

JACK: [*startled, and standing up stiffly*] I'm good, thank you, Mrs. Innes.

MAY: Polly says it's Uncle John.

JACK: [*with difficulty*] He'll be comin' back from Yanigee… I suppose Brum and the boys'll be with him.

MAY: You're knocked up.

JACK: [*sturdily*] Not a bit.

MAY: I shouldn't have let you go out after that killer.

JACK: [*gallantly*] Oh, the ridin's all right. Only I can't see as well as I used to; and Brumby turned out all the horses he wasn't takin' himself—except old Hero.

MAY: [*quickly*] One of the gins went with you, though?

JACK: Engi. Best gin on the place after cattle. She got the beast, really, and you should've heard her laugh when a white cockie, or somethin', frightened Hero. He pitched me off into a thorn bush—

MAY: There's the buggy. I can hear them pulling up.

BRUMBY: [*shouting*] Anybody at home?

JACK: [*as* MAY *turns to the door*] It's all right. It'll be all right.

Hearing BRUMBY'*s voice,* POLLY *reaches for a bottle of whisky on the shelf by the hearth and takes it with mug and quart pots to the table.*

MAY: How's the kettle, Polly? [*Looking around*] Oh… Well, Uncle John would like some tea…

She goes to the bench and POLLY *moves to help her.*

No, I'll make it myself, thanks.

BRUMBY: [*swaggering in, boisterously*] Hullo, Polly, where's my woman? Oh, there you are, May! [*As she stands off, staring at him*] Well, aren't you going to give your husband a kiss, like a respectable married woman? A peck on the cheek'll do…

MAY: [*coldly*] I'd rather not, thank you.

BRUMBY: Right. I'll kiss old Polly instead. [*Going to and kissing* POLLY] How's things, Polly?

He swings to the table and the whisky. POLLY *goes out.*

MAY: Uncle John! [*Clinging to him, and speaking under her breath*] I can't stand it. Truly, I can't. It's driving me out of my mind.

JOHN: That was over the fence, Brum.

BRUMBY: [*snarling and lifting his pot of whisky*] You keep y'r mouth shut. [*Putting the pot down and pouring again*] I've had enough of you jawrin' me head off.

MAY: You meant it for the best, Unc. But let me come home with you. Let me come home.

JACK: [*while* JOHN *is trying to soothe* MAY] How'd things go, Brum?

JOHN: They nearly didn't go, and [*with anger*] I wish to God, now, I'd let him stew in his own juice.

BRUMBY: [*sitting on the edge of the table and exhilarated by the whisky*] Lot you had to do with it.

JOHN: I had everything to do with it, that's all.

MAY *moves away to the bench to make tea for him.*

JACK: What?

JOHN: He'd've gone up for nine or ten years, for a dead cert'…

JACK: On the age of the girl?

JOHN: Told the magistrate himself, she was thirteen and three months.

JACK: You didn't do that, Brum?

JOHN: Got round the town before he went to court. Did my best to get him there sober, Jack, but it was no use.

BRUMBY: [*crowing and imitating the magistrate*] 'How can you say the girl's age is sixteen, Mr. Hallinan, when as a matter of fact, the defendant states the age of the girl to be thirteen years and three months? If he didn't know—wasn't sure—why should he say three months?'

JACK: Did you say she was sixteen, John?

JOHN: I did. That's what I reck'n her age is…

BRUMBY: [*continuing his recitation*] 'Oh,' says he, lyin' like a tripe hound. 'I know she's sixteen because I saw her. She was livin' with her people on the Creek first time I come through with cattle ten years ago. She was six or seven then—couldn't be less. I been on Nyedee ten years next January, and…'

JACK: That got him off, John.

> MAY *puts a cup of tea on the table beside* JOHN *and goes to the doorway, looking out but listening too.*

BRUMBY: [*enjoying his mimicry*] 'How do you account for the fact that Mr. Innes says the girl is thirteen years and three months, Mr. Hallinan? 'Oh, well, y'r worship,' says Mr. St. Anthony John Hallinan, 'he's been having a few drinks this mornin', and how much importance can you attach to anything a man says when he doesn't know what he's saying?' 'True, true.'

JACK: He don't deserve it, John.

BRUMBY: [*hilariously*] Discharged without a stain on me character!

JACK: It's more'n most men would do for you, Brum.

BRUMBY: Good old John. [*Pushing the bottle towards him*] Have a drink, John? But he's me uncle now, don't forget, Jack. We're relations be marriage.

JACK: How did the boys get on?

JOHN: Six months for assault.

BRUMBY: And one month for burglary, and breakin'–in and stealin'.

MAY: [*coming down to him*] Unc!

> JOHN *rises from the table and she throws her arms around him.*

You will take me home with you, won't you?

BRUMBY: [*savagely*] What are you crawlin' round him for?

JOHN: You'd better let her come back with me, Brumby.

BRUMBY: [*more sour and savage than he has been*] See here, John Hallinan, you can't have things both ways. You've got all you wanted out of me. You would have, I'd got to marry the girl… hush up any scandal. Marry her I did, and she's my woman. I won't have no more tellin' me what I ought to do.

MAY: [*distressfully*] Unkie!

BRUMBY: See here, May. [*Walking over and twisting her by the shoulder away from* JOHN] You stay here.

JACK: [*anxious to pacify everybody*] It's all right… It'll be all right.

BRUMBY: You got them calves, John?

JOHN: Yes… I got a couple of dozen calves, Brumby.

BRUMBY: Well, I reck'n, if you and me's not comin' to blows, you'd better get out—and quick, feller.

JOHN: [*with indignation*] If that's the way you're talkin'—

JACK: Don't be a fool, John.

BRUMBY: [*pouring himself out another drink*] No. Don't be a fool, John. Y'r not a fighting man. You know y'r not.

JOHN: You know I'm not. And what's more, we've got to talk this thing out. Peaceably.

BRUMBY: [*putting down his mug after having drunk*] We aren't going to talk no more.

JOHN: Then May's coming home with me.

BRUMBY: [*bashing him across the face*] It's a lie.

JACK: Brum!

JOHN *pitches off his coat and shapes up.*

JOHN: Come on then, let's have it.

MAY: Unkie! Unkie!

BRUMBY: [*to her*] You've asked for it.

Game as JOHN *is,* BRUMBY *pastes him unmercifully.*

JACK: For God's sake, Brum!

MAY: Make him stop. Oh…

BRUMBY: Goin' back, is she?

JACK: [*wrestling with* BRUMBY] Leave off. Y'll kill him, Brum.

BRUMBY: [*as* JOHN *falls*] Goin' back, is she? Bloody fool!

Returning to the table, he sits down on it and reaches for the whisky. MAY *and* JACK *go to* JOHN.

Goin' back, is she?

MAY: Is he dead, Mr. Carey?

JACK: He's all right. He'll be all right.

He goes to the table for whisky and pours some into a mug.

Polly!

Returning to JOHN, JACK *puts the mug to* JOHN*'s mouth.* POLLY *appears in the doorway.*

Water.

POLLY stares silently at JOHN, *goes to the hearth for a bucket of water and puts it down beside* JACK.

BRUMBY: [*slouching to the door and roaring*] Gingarra! Tommy! God damn and blast'm. No gettin' anything out of the bloody niggers on this place. Gingarra! Buck un–ma… quick feller… or I'll flay the hides off of you. [*As the natives appear*] John Hallinan wants to get a move on. Put his horses in and bring the buggy over.

Slamming his hat over his head and with a contemptuous look at the man on the floor, he goes out.

JACK: [*washing* JOHN'*s face with his own handkerchief*] He'll be all right.

JOHN: [*moving and moaning*] May!

MAY: [*on her knees beside him*] I'm here, Unc.

JACK: [*as* JOHN *sits up*] Y'r all right, John?

JOHN: [*dazedly, passing his hand over his head*] I ought to have known better.

JACK: 'Course you should, John.

JOHN: What am I goin' to do about her, Jack? God, I could blow my brains out for ever having brought her here. And then marrying her to the brute. But I thought it was for the best. I thought I'd got to see he married her.

JACK: Look here, John. If yer take my advice y'll leave things alone. Brum ain't unkind to his women…

JOHN: Prides himself on that, doesn't he?

JACK: He's rough as bags; but he'll treat Mrs. Innes proper. He's well–in too. Can give her anything she wants if she only handles him right.

MAY: [*passionately*] I hate him.

JACK: [*shrewdly*] I'm not so sure of that. I think he gets you… like the rest of 'em.

MAY: [*flinging away impatiently*] Oh!

BRUMBY: [*in the doorway*] Kerridge, me lord.

JACK: [*helping* JOHN *to the door*] She'll be all right, John. Don't you worry.

JOHN: You'll do what you can, I know, Jack.

JACK: 'Course I will.

JOHN: [*kissing* MAY] I've made a mess of this, darling. I thought…

MAY: [*drearily*] I understand, Unc. It can't be helped now.

JOHN: [*uneasily*] Try to make the best of it.

MAY: [*desperately*] I don't know! I don't know what I'll do.

JOHN: It's true, what Jack says. Brumby's generous in his own way; and he prides himself on treating women better than most men.

MAY: Good–bye, Unkie!

JOHN: Good–bye. [*Kissing her again*] Jack'll keep me posted how you are. [*As he goes out*] I'll send a boy over with books and papers every week.

JACK: [*calling after him*] Good–bye, John. She's all right. She'll be all right.

> *He comes back into the room,* BRUMBY *behind him;* MAY *is standing at the window on the left looking out.*

BRUMBY: Clear out, Jack.

> JACK *picks up his hat and steers his long creaking figure to the door again.* BRUMBY *turns to* POLLY *at the hearth.*

Scram! [*As she dawdles*] Get the hell out of this!

> POLLY *swings to the door, scowling.* MAY *moves to follow her, but he intercepts her.*

No, it's you I'm cuttin'–out.

> MAY *comes back into the room disconsolately, goes to the chair on the other side of the table and sits down.*

MAY: Well, what is it?

BRUMBY: [*following and gazing at her cynically, savagely*] Think I'm shook on you, don't you? You damned silvertail. You poor, sickly, miserable–lookin' creature.

MAY: Then why don't you let me go back to Nyedee?

BRUMBY: I'll never let you go back to Nyedee. What you've got to understand is, you're one of Brumby's mares. You gallop with the mob.

MAY: [*jumping up*] It's outrageous.

BRUMBY: You'll get feed and water—the best. A brumby leads his mares to good grass. I won't bother you when y'r with foal. Like you are now. You can go south, in a couple of months, mooch off, and choose your own place to lay down. There'll be money to do what you like till it's a fair thing to come back.

MAY: What if I don't come back?

BRUMBY: You'll come back, all right.

MAY: [*defiantly*] Will I? I'm not so sure of that. I was engaged to a man who was really fond of me when I came up here; and you—

BRUMBY: A brumby boss–horse don't allow his mare to be took off...

MAY: Until another shows him he's not the boss he thought he was?

BRUMBY: That's right.

MAY: [*desperately*] But if you're not keen on me—

BRUMBY: Got nothing to do with it.

MAY: Oh, how I hate men!

BRUMBY: And I hate women. Hate their silly, wimperin' palaver about love. Dressin' themselves up—plasterin' themselves with powder and scent till they stink like an Afghan. For why? To get men flutterin' round them—like you had all the men up here.

MAY: You don't know the meaning of love.

BRUMBY: Don't I? Love! I don't want to. [*Spitting*] See. I don't want to. Do y' know what love is? [*As she does not answer*] It's the smoke you blasted women put up to do men out of being plain, ordinary, decent male animals.

MAY: [*with disgust*] You mean love gets between you and...

BRUMBY: I mean what you call love's a god–damned sham.

MAY: All you care about's your filthy lusts.

BRUMBY: Here, [*taking her by the shoulder*] you keep your tongue off of talking like that. My lust's not filthy. It's natural. Makes me feel good. Like the rain... and the rivers runnin' when everything's dead and dry, up here.

MAY: [*drearily*] I suppose so.

BRUMBY: But I want youngsters. And a good home. You can make it what you like. Now the station's grown, there's the question

who's to get it when I'm gone. I want youngsters, and I want'm
thoroughbred. It's a damned insult to a man not to see children
about him.

MAY: Gins don't go in for child–bearing.

BRUMBY: The old men won't let 'em—if food's short. Look here, May,
it's goin' to make a lot of difference to me, havin' the kid. Give me
a chance, and we'll trot along well enough. I'll do anything to make
things right for you and the young 'un.

MAY: [*passionately*] I loathe the sight of you, this blasted country, and
everything in it.

BRUMBY: [*sardonically*] All right! Have it your own way.

WYLBA: [*prancing cheekily in the doorway*] Munyin bunna, nunki–
nunki, chungee–chungee.

She disappears.

MAY: She's not coming back here, is she?

BRUMBY: [*recovering his good humour and pose*] Where else'd she
go? She belongs here, doesn't she? Down at the camp.

WYLBA: [*putting her head in at the window, impishly*] W'alyee Mari,
booketerra, kundi–kundi, spa!

BRUMBY: [*exuberantly*] But Wylba isn't the only pebble on the plains.
Not by long chalks—There's Melanie at Koodgieda. I've only got
to send a rifle and couple of blankets to her old man, to get her when
I want her. [*Putting on the gramophone*] How's it for a bit of music?

A lively tune blares out. WYLBA *comes sneaking back, looks in
at the door, listening.*

But Wylba don't mind lettin' bygones be bygones, do you, Wylba?
Come on, Wylba, give us a step.

The little native girl dances forward. BRUMBY *prances with
her.* MAY *watches a moment, then with a gesture of defeat goes
out. Across the plains the sun is setting.* BRUMBY *'s laughter and*
WYLBA *'s shrill giggling mingle with the gay, harsh music of the
gramophone.*

CURTAIN

Abbreviations

1940   *Brumby Innes*, Perth 1940

A   a copy of 1940 containing Katharine
Prichard's manuscript alterations as
described in the Introduction

APPENDIX I

Notes on the Aboriginals in Brumby Innes

by Carl von Brandenstein

The Tribe and the Language

In her 1940 Preface (see p. 49), Katharine Susannah Prichard gives the name of the tribe as Gnulloonga, which becomes in modern transcription *Ngaala–warngga*, meaning the language (*warngga*) which uses the word *ngaala* to express the pronoun 'this'. The tribe speaking the *Ngaala* dialect is known to linguists as the South *Pandjima*. They form a link between the *Pandjima* proper in the north and the *Paljgu* in the east. Turee Creek, the station K.S.P. visited in 1927, is in the heart of South *Pandjima* territory.

The Music

Nothing had been published about Aboriginal singing in the north–west until an article by the present commentator appeared in *Hemisphere* in November 1969, entitled 'Tabi Songs of the Aborigines'. In the 1940 Preface, and also in the Foreword to *Coonardoo*, Katharine Prichard referred to corroboree songs as 'tabee'. The term *tabi*, however, is reserved for individual songs composed and performed by a solo singer or *Njinirri* (K.S.P.'s 'yinerrie') who accompanies himself by rhythmically scraping across the notches on his spear–thrower as on a rasp with a wooden fork, whereas a corroboree is either a sacred–secret or profane performance by the group. The only instrumental accompaniment to the singing is provided by two boomerangs. (Katharine Prichard's south–west term 'kylie' is imported to the north–west by the whites; the local terms are *wirra* or *wargoondi*.) The *Njinirri*, like our conductor, is in charge of the musical part only. The dance–master, like our choreographer, remains independent of the conductor and normally rehearses away from the *Njinirri*.

First Song

The first song is a typical *Ngalli* (Ngarlee) or 'prelude' to a corroboree.

It serves the purpose of filling time before the dancers are ready, or during intervals between different scenes. This *Ngalli* is in the Pandjima language. The translation (see p. 116) is free but mostly accurate.

[1940 has a note: 'The song, used as an invocation to the men who are to corroboree, is the song of a stranger in a strange land, describing what he sees.' Ed.]

Second Song

This is in *Ngaala–warngga* or *Njirrikudhu* (the language of the *Paljgu*). The *Naalu* (Narlu, Narloo), explained by K.S.P. as 'spirit, evil one', is neither a devil nor a ghost. The *Naalus* are mythical figures known all over the north–west under different names. They prefer the rocky hills of the Table Land and the Hamersley Ranges as their haunts, are human–like but an older race. Their toes are grown together; they have an enormous penis with a barbed hook as a head which, when not erect, is coiled around the waist many times, and when erect can stretch for miles underground to reach and hold unsuspecting women who might become pregnant by this approach. That is the reason for the women's outspoken fear of the *Naalu*. On the other hand, the *Naalus* carry individual names and some of them, like *Kanjoon*, are famous as inventors of the rules of song–making. They are also the guardians of localities and hunting grounds. A stranger has to appease them by squirting a few mouthfuls of water in the direction of the unknown terrain before entering.

The relation between a stranger and the *Naalus* is obviously the theme of the corroboree which Katharine Prichard took most conscientiously from authentic sources and revived in her play. There can be no doubt that the *Naalus* resemble closely in appearance and role the class of Greek woodland deities in human form with horse's or goat's tail and legs, the satyrs, who were likewise inventors of music and known by name (e.g., the famous and ill–fated Marsyas).

Katharine Prichard's translation of the *Naalu* verse is not quite exact. It should read:

> *Naalu! Naalu! tjirndu pannabia,*
> *Warrida munga marnda pannabia,*
> *Naalu kalla pu(y)unka(rr)ai, Naalu kinarra*
> *pu(y)unka(rr)ai.*

Nubai! taaniwalli Naalu wudimaru
Kalla pu(y)unka(rr)ai, kinarra pu(y)unka(rr)ai.

Translation:

Naalu! Naalu! The sun they have blurred,

The eagle's dark mount they have blurred,

With the grey haze of the *Naalu*'s fire, with their *Naalu*'s grey haze over the full moon.

You! Somewhere else, *Naalus*, you should run

With the grey haze of your fires, with your grey haze over the full moon.

These strong lines express the belief of the Aborigines that mist and haze in the hills are caused by the campfires of the *Naalus*.

Third Song

The third dancing scene is accompanied not by a song but by an 'intoned chant', typical of the work of a *Naalu* as composer. Instead of a melody we have here a strictly poetical and emphatically chanted metre in a set of two dactylic tetrameters. Thus:

Úbay ubáya he | pínna ha wáya,
Wárrala ngáya | -pínna ha wáya.

'*Ha*' and '*he*' are syllable fillers without meaning; their function is to ensure the correct metre. The text is difficult to establish from the free translation.

Katharine Susannah Prichard and the Aborigines

Katharine Prichard has assessed very well the relations, i.e., the mutual misunderstandings, between white and black. She did not bother much to be careful about expressing her disgust with the dubious role of the white man as conqueror and subsequently as over self–confident assimilator. It seems that she saw the plight of the Aboriginals in her early days, as she might have seen the Fijians or other vanquished people whom she either knew or had read about. She certainly stood up against racial discrimination generally. We must admit, however, that there is a great difference between loving people because one emphasises the human factors in common and concedes equal rights to all—an outlook fostered by urbanity—and respecting people in their own right, and for the difference of their race and culture and one's own, and consequently avoiding interference for good or bad if it is not asked for—an outlook rather of intellectual neo–nomads.

When it comes to analysing the degree of Katharine Prichard's understanding of Aboriginal man apart from his obvious conflict with white civilization and within his own set of culture values, it remains doubtful whether she was able to penetrate to the depth of the problem. It is perhaps a deplorable mark of her society that she, herself a keen student of foreign languages and determined to read the great masters of world literature in their own language, could not apply this principle to the Aboriginals because of her short acquaintance with the north–west. She sensed, but could not perceive fully, the dramatic power and beauty of true Aboriginal poetry as expressed in the *tabi* and corroboree songs of the hundreds of *Njinirris* whose art is doomed to extinction if the short–sighted aim of integration into a 'one culture, one language' uniformity is continued.

Another obstacle to Katharine Prichard's greater involvement in Aboriginal problems could be the fact that she was a woman, and so inevitably excluded from the man's world of the Aborigines. It is understandable then that her heroes were Polly and Coonardoo rather than the more vaguely drawn characters of Wongana, Mickina or Spider.

APPENDIX II

Glossary of Aboriginal words in Ngaala-warngga occurring in
Brumby Innes

Compiled by Carl von Brandenstein and incorporating manuscript notes by
Katharine Prichard in text A

Words in italics represent the modern spelling.

babba (*paba*), water.
badgee (*padji*), angry, wild.
balgarilla (*parlgarrala*), on the plain.
belyee mari (*piljimarri*), penis, puffy.
bina, hidden.
bita muna (*pidamanna*), fed up with.
booger (*purga*), chap, fellow.
booketera (*pugatharra*), stinker, one who stinks.
borki (*pu(y)unka(rr)ai*), grey smoke, haze; australite.
buckunma (*pakanma*), come here!
bun abbia (*pannabia*), they have twisted, blurred, thrown at it.

chungee chungee (*tjandji-tjandji*), jagged (penis?).
cootharra, cotharra (*kudharra*), two.

eeh-erm (*eh-eh*), confirmation (A: 'Eeh-erm is like our Mmm!').

gina-gina (*tjina-tjina*), dress.
Ginarra (*Tjinara*), male name.
gindoo (*tjirndu*), sun.

kala (*kalla*), fire, firewood.
kalla miah (*kalla-maya*), wood store, woodheap.
kinerra (*kinnara*), full moon.
ko, koo (*ku*), yes, derisively (A: 'a long hooting call of derision').
Koodgieda (*Kudjida*), fictitious station.

Kulliwarigo (*Kuliwarrigu*), meaning dubious.
kundi-kundi (*kurndai-kurndai?*), shame!
kuningmarra (*kaningmarra*), meaning dubious.
kurrie (*kurri*), young girl, virgin.

mardoo mardourie (*mardumardurrii*), it flattens, spreads out.
meetchie (*midjidji*), Mrs.
meta warra (*midda-wara*), pretty; white clothes.
miah (*maya*), European house or hut.
Mickina (*Mirrgina*), big one; male name.
movin (*maparn, mavarn*), charm, witchcraft.
mulba (*marlba*), man, mortal.
munda, murnda (*marnda*), stone, rock, hill, metal, money.
Munga (*Manga*), woman, or (*Munga*), dark, female name.
munga (*munga*), night, dark.
munyin bunna, minyin bunna (*manyinbana*), a filthy swear word.
    (A notes on p. 60, where this word first occurs, 'This defiance of
    Wylba's is in filthy language—quite untranslatable. So long as she
    hurls something at Brumby, it doesn't matter what she says.')
murda (*marda*), blood.
murda-murda (*mardamarda*), red, Sturt Pea.
murndoo (*murndo*), could be, perhaps.

nabi (*nabai,* from *nuvalai*), you fellows.
Narloo (*Naalu*), see notes on music.
noova (*nuva, njuba*), lover, spouse (A: 'a difficult word to translate.
    It means potential wife, and a woman with whom a man may have
    a sex relationship. The natives in this tribe actually use the word
    "lover", because the white people suggested it as nearest to lover,
    I think').
nuki-nuki (*nuggai*), loathsome, dangerous.
nunki-nunki (*ngangai-ngangai*), swearword.

piriyina (*pirriina*), having become the end.
punti (*parndi*), smell.

spa, an exclamation (A: '"spa" is spat out').

tanbura, cliff(?).
taniwali (*taaniwalli*), whither, (any)where to.
Tullamurra (*Tala-mara*), Healthy-hand, a female name.

ubi, **oobaya** (*ubaya*), mate.
uloo (*jurlu*), camp.

walygee booger (*waldji-purga*), false, bad chap.
walyinna (*waljina*), bad one, false one.
wanarloo (*wanarralu*), by a tall one; (*wanarra*), tall.
wandy (*warndi*), tail, penis; *wandy cloth*, a garment which covers the
  male pudenda.
wara lunghia bina (*warrala nga(rr)ibina*), in the void lying.
warieda (*warrida*), eagle-hawk.
warilla (*warri-la*), on the ground.
wiah (*waya*), no.
winning arra(s) (*win ingkarra*), whirlwinds.
Wongana (*Wankana*), Lively one, male name.
wongie (*warngkai*), talk.
wudimaru (*wudimaru*), run away, go home!

yaberoo (*yaburru*), north.
Yanigee (*Yannidji*), a fictitious town.
yienda (*njinda*), you (singular).
yiendie (*yindii*), goes down, slopes.
yinerrie (*njinirri*), musician, composer.
yukk-eye (*yaggarri, yaggai*), exclamation of surprise or sudden pain.

APPENDIX III

The Song Bid Me To Love

The song *Bid Me To Love* was published by Ascherberg, Hopwood & Crew, London (n.d.). Words by Clifton Bingham, music by D'Auvergne Barnard.

> I do not ask for the heart of thy heart,
> I do not bid thee remain or depart,
> Let me but love thee and I will not plead
> Aught save to follow where e'er thou dost lead.
>
> All that I ask for is all that may be,
> All that thou carest to give unto me;
> I am content to be this unto thee,
> To love thee for ever, love thee for ever and ever.
> I am content to be this unto thee,
> To love thee for ever and ever.
>
> Let me but live in the light of thy face,
> Find in thy heart and thy being a place;
> Though it be low at thy feet, being there
> I can my homage more fitly declare, my homage declare.
>
> Then, as the sunflower looks up to the light,
> Sad in its absence and glad in its sight,
> I can look up to thee, morning and night,
> And love thee for ever, love thee for ever and ever.
> I can look up to thee, morning and night,
> And love thee for ever and ever.

BID ME TO LOVE.

Words by CLIFTON BINGHAM.   Music by D'AUVERGNE BARNARD.

love thee and I will not plead Aught save to
f
Ped.
fol - low wher - e'er thou dost lead. All that I
allargando.
ff
f
f
colla voce.
Ped.
a tempo.
ask for is all that may be All that thou
ff
a tempo.
mp
Ped.
car - est to give un - to me; I am con -
con espress:
Ped.

cres - cen - - do. ff
tent .... to be this un - to thee To
cres - - cen - do.
Ped. *
mp con espress.
love thee for .... ev - er love thee for
ff mp
Ped. * Ped. *
ev - - er .... and ev - - er I am con -
f
tent .... to be this un - to thee .... To
f
Ped.

Rall:
love thee for ev - er and ev - - - -
Rall:
8
er!
mf
a tempo
Led.
*
quicker.
Let me but
Led.
*
live .... in the light of thy face, Find in thy
quicker.

heart... and thy being a place; Though it be low.......... at thy feet being

there I can my hom _ age more fit _ ly de _ clare, my

hom _ age .... de _ clare; Then, as the sun _ flow'r looks up to the

light, Sad in its ab _ sence and glad in its sight, I can look

cres - cen - - do.
ff
up to thee, morning and night,
And love thee for ....
cres - - cen - - do.
ff
con espress:
mp
ev - er, love thee for ev - er.......... and ev - er, I can look
mp
Ped.
Rall:
up .... to thee, morning and night,.................. And love thee for ev - er and
f
Rall: mp
Ped.
morendo.
ev - - er.
pp
Cres
f
Ped.
Ped.

BIBLIOGRAPHY

AND

NOTES

Katharine Susannah Prichard: Select Bibliography
(with special reference to her dramatic writing)

PLAYS

Brumby Innes (Paterson's Press, Perth 1940)

The Pioneers, included in *Best Australian One–Act Plays*, ed. William Moore and T. Inglis Moore (Angus and Robertson, Sydney 1937)

In manuscript:

The Burglar: One-act, first produced by William Moore and Louis Esson, Melbourne 1909

A Miracle in the Street of Refugees: unproduced, c. 1910

Her Place: One-act, first produced by the Actresses' Franchise League, London 1913

For Instance: One-act, first produced by the Actresses' Franchise League, London 1914. (No copy traced.)

The Great Man: Three-act comedy, first produced by the Pioneer Players, Melbourne 1923

The Great Strike: unproduced, c. 1931

Women of Spain: One-act, first produced by the Workers Art Guild, Perth 1937

Forward One: One-act, first produced by the Workers Art Guild, Perth 1935

Penalty Clause: Three-act drama, first produced by the Workers Art Guild, Perth 1940

Deakin: unproduced, 1951

Good Morning: One-act sketch, first produced by the New Theatre of W.A., Perth 1955

Persephone's Baby: unproduced, c. 1955

NOVELS
First editions only:
The Pioneers (Hodder and Stoughton, London 1915)
Windlestraws (Holden and Hardingham, London 1916)
Black Opal (Heinemann, London 1921)
Working Bullocks (Cape, London 1926)
Wild Oats of Han (Angus and Robertson, Sydney 1928)
Coonardoo (Cape, London 1928)
Haxby's Circus (Cape, London 1930)
Intimate Strangers (Cape, London 1937)
Moon of Desire (Cape, London 1941)
The Roaring Nineties (Cape, London 1946)
Golden Miles (Cape, London 1948)
Winged Seeds (Australasian Publishing Co., Sydney 1950)
Subtle Flame (Australasian Book Society, Sydney 1967)

AUTOBIOGRAPHY
Child of the Hurricane (Angus and Robertson, Sydney 1964)

COLLECTED SHORT STORIES
Kiss on the Lips and Other Stories (Cape, London 1932)
Potch and Colour (Angus and Robertson, Sydney 1944)
N'Goola (Australasian Book Society, Melbourne 1959)
On Strenuous Wings (Seven Seas, Berlin 1965), ed. Joan Williams
Happiness (Angus and Robertson, Sydney 1967)

SELECTED ARTICLES
'Some Thoughts on Australian Literature', *The Realist Writer* No. 15, June 1964
'Some Perceptions and Aspirations', *Southerly*, Vol. 28 No, 4 (1968) pp. 235–244
'Our Dramatic Resources', *Prompt* (journal of the Canberra Repertory Society) 1955

WRITINGS ON KATHARINE SUSANNAH PRICHARD

Drake-Brockman, Henrietta, *Australian Writers and their Work: Katharine Susannah Prichard* (Oxford University Press, Melbourne 1967)

'K. S, Prichard: The Colour in her Work', *Southerly*, Vol. 14 No. 4 (1953), pp. 214–219

Franklin, Miles, in *Laughter Not for a Cage* (Angus and Robertson, Sydney 1956)

Grattan, C. Hartley, 'Readers and Writers Down Under', *The New York Times Book Review*, 22nd June 1947

Green, H. M., *A History of Australian Literature*, Vol. 2, 1923–1950 (Angus and Robertson, Sydney 1961)

Hewett, Dorothy, 'Excess of Love', *Overland*, No. 43, 1969/70 (Comment *Overland* No. 44, 1970)

Holburn, Muir, 'Katharine Susannah Prichard', *Meanjin Quarterly*, Vol. 10 No, 3, 1951

Lindsay, Jack, 'The Novels of Katharine Susannah Prichard', *Meanjin Quarterly*, Vol. 20 No. 4, 1961

'Reply to Ellen Malos', *Meanjin Quarterly*, Vol. 22 No. 1, 1963

Malos, Ellen, 'Some Major Themes in the Novels of Katharine Susannah Prichard', *Australian Literary Studies* No. 1, 1963

'Jack Lindsay's Essay on Katharine Susannah Prichard's Novels', *Meanjin Quarterly*, Vol. 22 No. 1, 1963

Palmer, Vance, *Louis Esson and the Australian Theatre* (Georgian House, Melbourne 1948)

Rees, Leslie, *The Making of Australian Drama* (Angus and Robertson, Sydney 1973)

Throssell, Ric, *Wild Weeds and Wind Flowers* (Angus and Robertson, Sydney 1976)

Wilkes, G. A., 'The Novels of K. S. Prichard', *Southerly*, Vol. 14 No. 4, 1953

Williams, Justina (Joan), 'Rage that Engenders', *Southerly*, Vol. 32 No. 1, 1972

Williams, Margaret, 'Natural Sexuality, Katharine Prichard's Brumby Innes', *Meanjin Quarterly*, Vol. 32 No. 1, 1973

Notes

Preface
1. *The Australian*, 11th November 1972.
2. *The Herald*, Melbourne, 11th August 1914.
3. 'Some Perceptions and Aspirations', *Southerly*, Vol. 28 No. 4 (1968), p. 237.
4. 'Our Dramatic Resources', *Prompt*, magazine of the Canberra Repertory Society, 1955.
5. 'The Cooboo', included in *Kiss on the Lips* (Cape, London 1932).
6. Letter from Louis Esson to Vance Palmer, 29th November 1927, quoted in *Louis Esson and the Australian Theatre* by Vance Palmer (Georgian House, Melbourne 1948), pp. 90–1. There is no trace of the additional act referred to by Louis Esson. If it was ever written I presume that it was included in the 1940 edition of the play revised by K.S.P. from which the present version is taken.
7. 'Natural Sexuality: Katharine Prichard's Brumby Innes', by Margaret Williams, *Meanjin Quarterly*, Vol. 32 No. 1 (1973), p. 92.
8. The origins and interpretations of *Intimate Strangers* are more fully explored in my biography of Katharine Susannah Prichard, *Wild Weeds and Wind Flowers*.
9. *The West Australian*, 13th September 1940.
10. *Australian Writers and their Work: Katharine Susannah Prichard* (Oxford University Press, Melbourne 1967), p. 30.
11. *The Making of Australian Drama*, by Leslie Rees (Angus & Robertson, Sydney 1973).

Introduction
1. *Coonardoo* (Angus & Robertson, Sydney 1957), p. 203.
2. *Child of the Hurricane* (Angus & Robertson, Sydney 1964), p. 257.
3. *Intimate Strangers* (Cape, London 1937), p. 83: Rachel. "But you know every woman over forty needs a lover. You're a fool to let Greg play about and run to seed yourself... let him see he's not the only man on earth you're interested in."
4. 'Against Indifference', by Charles Webbe. Also called 'More love or more disdain' in the *Oxford Book of English Verse*, ed. Arthur Quiller-Couch (Oxford University Press, 1900).

Glossary of Colloquialisms and Local Terms

Abo, a pejorative abbreviation of Aboriginal.

Banksia, an Australian genus of shrubs and trees (family Proteaceae) with bracted spikes of yellow or pink flowers which are followed by a woody, conelike cluster of fruits. *Banksia man*, a toy made from the banksia cone (see May Gibbs' classic children's story, *The Adventures of Snugglepot and Cuddiepie*).

Bingee (from a New South Wales aboriginal dialect), belly.

Breakway, **Breakaway**, a North–west term for a depression caused by erosion.

Brumby, a wild horse; *brumby cattle*, stock which have run wild and deteriorated in condition.

Butcher bird (Cracticus torquatus), considered by many to be Australia's finest song–bird, found throughout the continent.

Bundle, to drop one's, to panic, to give up hope.

Castlereagh, an inland river in New South Wales, rising in the Great Dividing Range and flowing into the Darling River.

Chookie, chicken.

Cleanskin, an unbranded head of cattle.

Cock–eyed bob, a North–west term for cyclone; in *Brumby Innes*, a man's nickname.

Cocki, cockatoo.

Crack hardy, to put on a brave face against misfortune or suffering.

Crook, ill.

Desert pea, Sturt's desert pea (cleanthus formosus).

Dust up, a fight; a melee.

Illawarra, a fertile region around Lake Illawarra, on the coast south of Sydney.

Kangaroo dog, also called bush greyhound, a breed of dog developed for hunting kangaroos and dingoes.

Karrara, a fictional station.

Killer, a beast to be killed for meat.

Koodgieda, a fictional town.

Kylie (from Aboriginal dialect), boomerang.

Mardourie, a fictional town.

Marthaga, a fictional river.

Monte, **monty**, a certainty, a safe thing.

Mulga, a variety of native tree (acacia aneura) often used to mean a general area of scrub.

Mundi, a fictional town.

Pink-eye, an infectious eye disease which afflicts both men and animals; *to go pink–eye*, probably to malinger.

Rusty, to cut up, to lose one's temper.

Silvertail, a member of the privileged class.

Skoot, liquor; *on the skoot*, on a drinking bout.

Square, fair, just; *square talk*, blunt talking; or in a pejorative sense, sermonising.

Sting, whisky; or more generally, spirits.

Wash-away, erosion caused by flooding.

Well-in, well established.

Yanigee, a fictional town.

Yarder, a horse which habitually escapes from its yard by jumping the rails.

Yarraman, an outlaw horse or wildly behaved station buck; in *Bid Me To Love*, a horse's name.

Textual Annotations

Throughout the following annotations 1940 will signify the edition of *Brumby Innes* published in that year by Paterson's Press, Perth; and A will signify the revised copy of that edition described in the Introduction to the 1974 edition, (iv) The Text, on page xxxi, which provides the text for the present edition.

ACT ONE

pp. 67–70: Several lines have been deleted in A from the first two songs in the corroboree, as have the translations incorporated into the text of 1940. In addition, A numbers the songs in the margin, an annotation which emphasises the three distinct stages of the corroboree.

p. 67 l. 26: First song: (*Then... each time.*, 1940:

WONGANA: (*women and children singing with him*)

       Balgarilla mardoo mardourie yiendie warilla,
       Piriyina murda tanbura munda wunarloo;
       Kuningmarra weeindie my babba yaberoo,
       Kuningmarra weeindie kulliwarigo.

       The great plain slopes gradually to a bluff and cliffy range,
       Coming from a long way off
       The whole falling away to a pool of water with reeds growing
          beside it.
       (The first line is sung twice, the second five times, the third twice, the last once; but each time a line is repeated the key varies.)

p. 68 l. 33 etc.: narloo] 1940 has 'narlu' throughout. A notes: "pronounced Narloo—rolling the 'r's".

p. 68 l. 34: Second Song: *The... before.*], 1940:

WOMEN:

       Narlu, narlu... gindoo bun abbi

Warrienda munga murnda bun abbi
Narlu… kala borki… narlu kinerra borki.
Nabi, tani wali narlu wudi maru kala borki, kinerra borki.
Narlu (Spirit—evil one)… the sun has gone;
The eagle hawk has flown away to the dark hills.
Narlu… smoke of the fire… smoke of the moon,
You fellows, tell the narlu to go whither the firelight goes, and
the smoke of the moon.

p. 69 l. 20: *The first… before.*], 1940: (*To the end.*) Not altered in A.
p. 69 l. 30–p.70 l. 7 ff.: Third Song.
   1940 gives the following translation, not deleted in A:
   Mate! Mate! hidden… held away in secret,
   We have been in hiding… held away.
p. 69 ll. 26-27: *old… dirty*] not in 1940
p. 70 l. 17: No,] not in 1940. A notes: "Wiah! means No! But Wylba's shrieks may well be kept to Wiah. It's got a wilder sound. Doesn't really matter what she says, so long as she wails and screams!"
p. 70 l. 23: camp] 1940: uloo)
p. 70 l. 29: angry] 1940: badgee (*angry*)
p. 70 l. 29: camp] 1940: uloo (*native camp*)
p. 70 l. 31: roaring] 1940: *stupidly*
p. 70 l. 35: angry] 1940: badgee
p. 71 l. 6: girl] 1940: kurrie
p. 71 l. 21: Promised one] 1940: Noova (*lover*) maybe
p. 71 l. 23: I'll] 1940: I

ACT TWO

p. 74 l. 3: Eeh–erm] 1940: Eeh–erm. (*yes*)
p. 74 l. 6: wongie] 1940: wongie (*tell*)
p. 74 l. 9: [*morosely*]… talkin'] 1940: Wongie–wongie
p. 74 l. 13: Father… baby.] 1940: Mickina noova.
p. 74 l. 16: He's… eh?] 1940: His lover?
p. 74 l. 18: She's… lovers?] 1940: Plenty of lovers, eh?
p. 74 l. 31: mob… to] 1940: mob of niggers comin' to
p. 75 l. 14: doin'] 1940: doing
p. 76 l. 9: *into*] 1940: *to*

p. 76 l. 30: koo] 1940: ko

p. 77 l. 1: yer] 1940: you. In most cases where 'yer' occurs in this text, A has altered 1940's 'you', 'your' or 'you're'. It has not been considered necessary to note each instance of this revision individually.

p. 77 l. 6: yer are] 1940: you're

p. 77 l. 15: charm] 1940: movin (*charm*)

p. 77 l. 28: y'll... y'bargain] 1940: you'll... you bargain

p. 78 ll. 10, 20: doin'... mornin'] 1940: doing... morning

p. 78 l. 23: I] not in 1940

p. 78 l. 34 : camp] 1940: uloo

p. 79 l. 2: No] 1940: Wiah

p. 79 l. 4: Scared eh] not in 1940

p. 79 ll. 14-15: Hallinan's... be... He'll] 1940: He's... by... I'll

p. 79 ll. 26-29: *looks... over him.*] 1940: *looks anxiously at the native on the bunk, returns to pull the blanket over him. Horses pull up beyond the verandah posts.*)

p. 80 l. 11: , miss] not in 1940

p. 80 l. 13: *blood*] 1940: *native*

p. 80 l. 15: [*cracking... always*] not in 1940

p. 80 l. 27: [*nervous... apologetic*] not in 1940

p. 81 l. 3: *eyeing*] 1940: *eyes on*

p. 81 l. 4: natives] 1940: niggers. In A, 'abos' was first substituted, then scored out.

p. 81 ll. 6-8: *At... explanation*] not in 1940

p. 81 l. 9: [*boisterously*] not in 1940

p. 81 l. 34: skin... nose] 1940: how

p. 82 ll. 4-5: here,... too, he] 1940: here, too, Ted was sayin' he

p. 83 l. 11: [*dryly*] not in 1940

p. 83 l. 12: [*to... attention*] not in 1940

p. 83 l. 18: [*jocosely*] not in 1940

p. 83 l. 23: [*refusing whisky*] not in 1940

p. 83 l. 25: [WYLBA... *wailing.*] not in 1940

p. 84 l. 8: [*chuckling*] not in 1940

p. 84 l. 19: *Laughter.*] not in 1940

p. 84 l. 22: [*gruffly*] not in 1940

p. 84 l. 30: [*chuckling*] not in 1940

p. 84 l. 33: [*apologetically*] not in 1940

p. 85 l. 17: [*uproariously*] not in 1940
p. 85 l. 25: agen] 1940: again
p. 86 l. 18: Oh… you.] 1940: Sing 'the Old Jig–Jog', Mr. Carey. Oh, do, I'd love to hear you sing it.
p. 86 l. 21: ridin'] 1940: riding
p. 87 l. 4: Go… please!] 1940: Oh, do, Mr. Carey.
p. 88 l. 15: She] not in 1940
p. 88 l. 18: [*slowly and clearly,*] not in 1940
p. 88 l. 24: [*derisively*] not in 1940
p. 88 l. 28: [*guilelessly*] not in 1940
p. 88 l. 36: the branded… in] 1940: the calf you had branded in
p. 89 l. 3: WYLBA… *now.*] not in 1940
p. 89 l. 6: [*amazed*] not in 1940
p. 89 l. 7: [*flatly*] not in 1940
p. 89 l. 9: MICKINA] 1940: *The boy*
p. 89 l. 15: [*jocosely*] not in 1940
p. 89 l. 19: [*with… admiration*] not in 1940
p. 89 l. 35: watching] 1940: watchin'
p. 90 l. 1: running] 1940: runnin'
p. 90 l. 9: *laughter*] 1940: *giggling*
p. 90 l. 20: Dirty dog] 1940: Balyi marl
p. 90 ll. 31-32: the boys] 1940: they
p. 91 l. 10: [*laughing*] not in 1940
p. 91 l. 17: with you] 1940: yienda (*you*)
p. 91 l. 18: [*puzzled*] not in 1940
p. 91 l. 24: Fed up] 1940: Bita muna
p. 91 l. 27: Pretty young girl… women] 1940: Meta warra kurrie (*Pretty young girl*)… Wylba… (*looking at* MAY) cootharra (*two*) women
p. 91 ll. 31-32: Niggers… station] 1940: They
p. 91 ll. 36-37: stand for niggers] 1940: stand niggers
p. 92 l. 8: a bit… brandin'] 1940: it
p. 93 l. 5: [*genially*] not in 1940
p. 93 l. 14: [*flirtatiously*] not in 1940
p. 93 l. 17: [*gaily*] not in 1940
p. 93 I. 18: I] not in 1940
p. 93 l. 20: [*teasing him*] not in 1940. The original insertion here was '(*baiting him*)'.

p. 93 l. 23: women are] 1940: women's
p. 94 l. 4: *nearer,*] 1940: *into the room*
p. 94 l. 12: MAY... *alarmed.*] not in 1940
p. 94 l. 14: never... tell] 1940: can never tell
p. 94 l. 16: over... fence] 1940: badgee
p. 94 l. 25: I... you] 1940: Virgin
p. 94 l. 30: [*scared*] not in 1940
p. 95 l. 4: [*coquettishly,*] not in 1940
p. 95 l. 8: aren't] 1940: ain't
p. 95 l. 16: , *but yielding*] 1940: *furiously*
p. 95 ll. 17-18: [*laughing... bunk*] 1940: (*embracing her roughly*).
    In A, 'buckin' a bit' was first altered to 'playin' up', then
    reinstated.

ACT THREE

p. 96 l. 25: Two] 1940: Cotharra
p. 97 l. 3: Murndoo] not in 1940
p. 97 l. 17: Do... hear?] not in 1940
p. 99 l. 2: Angry... Brumby] 1940: Bad tempered. An original revision
    reads: 'Angry with Brumby about something?'
p. 99 l. 3: Boys come] 1940: Come
p. 99 ll. 5-6: *up... yere*] 1940: *up in her own language*) Brumby buck
    un ma uloo, take Wylba yienda miah.
p. 99 l. 8: [*emphatically*]... Wylba.] 1940: (*heavily, doubtfully*)
    Brumby badgee uloo... take Wylba yienda miah.
p. 99 l. 9: the camp] 1940: uloo
p. 99 l. 13: is... she] 1940: , little girl
p. 99 l. 14: Eeh-erm] not in 1940. The actual insertion in A reads 'Eh-
    rmn'.
p. 99 ll. 19-20: What... out!] 1940: Yienda, wudi maru kalla miah!
    (*You go to wood heap*) Wudi maru, wudi maru, kala miah.
p. 99 l. 23: here] 1940: this
p. 99 l. 30: *power*] not in 1940
p. 99 ll. 34-35: POLLY... *out.*] not in 1940
p. 100 l. 8: dress] 1940: gina-gina
p. 100 l. 21: Young man] 1940: mulka (*young man*)
p. 100 ll. 24, 31: lover] 1940: noova

p. 100   l. 33: No] 1940: Wiah

p. 100   l. 35: [*coming… you!*] 1940: (*advancing threateningly*) Wudi maru kala miah!

p. 101   l. 18: little… dress] 1940: gina-gina

p. 101   ll. 28-29: help… Warrarie.] 1940: help Polly kill and skin that beast anyhow… Better go and kill that beast, Polly.

p. 101   l. 30: *red print*] 1940: *blue dungaree*

p. 101   l. 30: Yukk-eye] 1940: Eeh-erm

p. 101   l. 32: *material*] 1940: *dungaree*

p. 102   l. 3: Pretty… Pretty] 1940: Meta warra (*pretty*)… meta warra

p. 102   l. 20: go… killer] 1940: do it

p. 102   l. 28: MAY… up.] not in 1940

p. 102   l. 29: [*shouting*] Anybody] 1940: (*shouting outside as the dusty rattle-trap of a four-wheeled buggy draws up beyond the verandah*) Anybody

p. 102   l.30: [*as… turns*] 1940: (MAY *turning*

p. 103   l. 7: [*coldly*] not in 1940

p. 103   l. 31: my] 1940: me

p. 104   l. 13: *his mimicry*] 1940: *himself*

p. 104   l. 20: [*hilariously*] not in 1940

p. 104   l. 24: be] 1940: by

p. 105   l. 17: aren't] 1940: ain't

p. 105   l. 25: [*to her*] not in 1940

p. 105   l. 30: [*wrestling… Brum.*] 1940: Leave off… can't y'r?

p. 106   l. 35: 'em] 1940: them

p. 107   l. 9: Try] 1940: You'll try

p. 107   l. 10: [*desperately*] not in 1940

p. 107   l. 13: Unkie] 1940: Uncie

p. 107   l. 24: Scram!] 1940: Wudi maru.

p. 107   l. 32: don't you? You] 1940: don't you? Think I want you… You

p. 108   l. 11: [*defiantly*] not in 1940

p. 108   l. 16: on me—] 1940: on me—don't want me…

p. 108   l. 17: with it] 1940: with it. You're one of my mares. You run with the mob.

p. 108   l. 30: All… your] 1940: And your

p. 108   l. 34: up here.] 1940: up here. It's your messy love business that's wrong, sickly, shinanickin'... I got nothing to do with it. You did your damnedest to get me goin'. You deserve what you got.

p. 108   ll. 36-37: And... like.] not in 1940

p. 109   l. 5: men... food's short.] 1940: women... they can help it.

p. 109   l. 8: young 'un] 1940: kid

p. 109   l. 11: [*sardonically*]... right!] not in 1940

p. 109   l. 17: camp] 1940: uloo

p. 109   I. 20: [*exuberantly*] not in 1940

9 7 8 1 7 6 0 6 2 1 9 1 9